KNOWLEDGE
AND EXPERIENCE

in the philosophy of F. H. Bradley

KNOWLEDGE AND EXPERIENCE

in the philosophy of F. H. Bradley

by

T. S. ELIOT

COLUMBIA UNIVERSITY PRESS

New York

Columbia University Press Morningside Edition 1989
Columbia University Press
New York

Copyright © 1964 by T. S. Eliot
Reprinted by arrangement with Farrar, Straus & Giroux, Inc.

Library of Congress Cataloging-in-Publication Data
Eliot, T. S. (Thomas Stearns), 1888–1965.
Knowledge and experience in the philosophy of F. H. Bradley.
Reprint. Originally published: New York : Farrar, Straus, 1964.
Originally presented as the author's thesis (Ph.D.)—Harvard University, 1916.
Bibliography: p.   Includes index.
1. Bradley, F. H. (Francis Herbert), 1846–1924.   I. Title.
B1618.B74E48   1989   192   89-9882
ISBN 0-231-07150-7 (alk. paper)
ISBN 0-231-07151-5 (pbk. : alk. paper)

Printed in the United States of America

*Casebound editions of Columbia University Press books are Smyth-sewn
and are printed on permanent and durable acid-free paper*

TO MY WIFE
who urged me to publish
this essay

Preface

From October 1911 until June 1914 I was a student in the Harvard Graduate School as a candidate for the degree of Doctor of Philosophy. This degree was to be attained in three stages: at the end of the second year by Preliminary Examinations in which one was tested in all the branches of philosophy which one had studied, and in the ability to translate French and German philosophical work into English; later by the presentation of a dissertation on a subject approved by the heads of the department; and finally a *viva*, in which the aspirant defended his thesis and was again tested for his command of logic, psychology and the history of philosophy.

The dissertation which is here published for the first time, was prepared during those years and during a year in which, thanks to the award of a Sheldon Travelling Fellowship by Harvard University, I was at Merton College as a pupil of Harold Joachim, the disciple of Bradley who was closest to the master. To Harold Joachim I owe a great deal: the discipline of a close study of the Greek text of the *Posterior Analytics*, and, through his criticism of my weekly papers, an understanding of what I wanted to say and of how to say it. On going down from Oxford in 1915 I made the decision to stay in England, and had to seek a source of livelihood. From the autumn of 1915 until the end of 1916 I earned my living as a schoolmaster. I did not, however, abandon immediately the intention of fulfilling the conditions for the doctor's degree. Harvard had made it possible for me to go to Oxford for a year; and this return at least I owed to Harvard. So, amongst my other labours, I completed the first draft of my dissertation, and despatched it across the Atlantic for the judgment of the Harvard Department of Philosophy. In April 1916, when this work was completed, I was a junior master at the Highgate Junior School.

9

Preface

So much for the origins of this study of the theory of knowledge according to the philosophy of Francis Herbert Bradley. I did not return to Harvard to complete the requirements for the doctor's degree, and I did not see that University again for seventeen years after I had left it. Nor did I give any further thought to this dissertation after learning that it had been officially approved. A few years ago Professor Hugh Kenner of California in his book *The Invisible Poet* drew attention to it in a chapter on my debt to Bradley. My curiosity, however, was first stimulated by a visit from Professor Anne Bolgan of the University of Alaska, who had read the script in the Harvard University archives, and had obtained, with my permission, a photostatic copy. She had also seen there the carbon copy of a letter to me from Professor J. H. Woods written shortly after my dissertation had been presented, in which he said that Josiah Royce, the *doyen* of American philosophers, had spoken of it 'as the work of an expert'. Mr William Jackson, curator of the Houghton Library at Harvard, supplied me with a photostatic copy of the text (the original typescript being, of course, the property of the University).

To Professor Bolgan, who has made a close study of this essay, I am deeply indebted. She has read the present text and made important corrections and suggestions; she has most painstakingly edited the text. We have endeavoured, however, only to remove such errors and blemishes as appear to have been due to carelessness or haste. She has also checked my references (as far as is now possible) and has prepared a select bibliography, the index, and valuable notes.

I wish also to thank Mr Peter Heath of the University of St Andrews, for translating the passages quoted from German authors.

Forty-six years after my academic philosophizing came to an end, I find myself unable to think in the terminology of this essay. Indeed, I do not pretend to understand it. As philosophizing, it may appear to most modern philosophers to be quaintly antiquated. I can present this book only as a curiosity of biographical interest, which shows, as my wife observed at once, how closely

Preface

my own prose style was formed on that of Bradley and how little it has changed in all these years. It was she who urged me to publish it; and to her I dedicate it.

There is evidently a page or so missing from chapter VI: the gap occurs after the last sentence of the paragraph which here ends at the top of page 146. What may at first appear more serious is the loss of one or several pages of the conclusion of the essay. The last page of the typescript ends with an unfinished sentence: *For if all objectivity and all knowledge is relative.* . . . I have omitted this exasperating clause: it is suitable that a dissertation on the work of Francis Herbert Bradley should end with the words 'the Absolute'. Mr. Jackson tells me that these pages were missing when the script came into his care. This does not seem to me to matter: the argument, for what it is worth, is there.

But at Professor Bolgan's suggestion I have appended, as partial compensation for the loss of the concluding page or pages, two essays which I wrote in 1916, and which appeared in *The Monist*, a philosophical periodical published in Chicago. It was Philip Jourdain, the British correspondent of that journal (to whom, I remember, I had been introduced by Bertrand Russell) who kindly commissioned these articles. They appeared in a number devoted to the celebration of the bi-centenary of the death of Leibniz.

The original title of this dissertation was *Experience and the Objects of Knowledge in the Philosophy of F. H. Bradley* with the sub-title *A thesis submitted in partial fulfilment of the requirements for candidates for the doctorate of philosophy in philosophy at Harvard University.*

T.S.E.

Contents

CHAPTER I

On Our Knowledge of
Immediate Experience

It is not my intention in the present paper to cover the whole field of epistemology, or even to hint at the existence of many questions of which my subject seems to demand some discussion. The formation of general ideas, the theory of judgment and inference, probability and the validity of knowledge, fall outside the scope of my attempt. And the problem of error will seem to receive very slight treatment. In the present chapter I wish to take up Bradley's doctrine of 'immediate experience' as the starting point of knowledge. Then the rest of the essay will occupy itself with the development of subject and object out of immediate experience, with the question of independence, and with the precise meaning of the term 'objectivity'.

Bradley uses the term 'experience' and the term 'feeling' almost interchangeably, both in *Appearance* and in the essay 'On Our Knowledge of Immediate Experience'* which is the most important *locus* for my present chapter. In the use of these terms we must observe the greatest caution. We must be on guard, in the first place, against identifying experience with consciousness, or against considering experience as the adjective of a subject. We must not confuse immediate experience with sensation, we must not think of it as a sort of panorama passing before a reviewer, and we must avoid thinking of it as the content or substance of a mind. And 'feeling' we must remember, is a term of very wide application, so that in some of its quite legitimate uses it is cer-

* In *Essays on Truth and Reality* (referred to as *Truth and Reality* in subsequent notes).

tainly not identical with 'experience'. We must accustom ourselves to 'feeling' which is not the feeling of psychologists, though it is in a way continuous with psychological feeling. And when we are told (*Appearance*, p. 406) that feeling is 'the immediate unity of a finite psychical centre' we are not to understand that feeling is merely the feeling *of* a mind or consciousness. 'It means for me, first, the general condition before distinctions and relations have been developed, and where as yet neither any subject nor object exists. And it means, in the second place, anything which is present at any stage of mental life, in so far as that is only present and simply is. In this latter sense we may say that everything actual, no matter what, must be felt; but we do not call it feeling except so far as we take it as failing to be more.' (*Appearance*, pp. 406–7.)

Keeping these quotations in mind, we turn at once to the words with which the whole theory is summed up in the essay to which I have referred. Experience, we are told, 'is not a stage which shows itself at the beginning and then disappears, but it remains at the bottom throughout as fundamental. And further, remaining, it contains in itself every development which in a sense transcends it. Nor does it merely contain all developments, but in its own way it acts as their judge.'[1] In these words we have expressed the whole difference between Bradley's view of experience and those of certain other contemporary philosophers. For, in the first place, immediate experience is not at any stage of consciousness merely a presentation which can be isolated from other elements also present or subsequent in consciousness. It is not 'sense-data' or sensations, it is not a stream of feeling which, as merely felt, is an attribute of the subject side only and must in some way be 'related' to an external world. And it is not, lastly, more pure or more immediate in the animal or the infant mind than in the mind of the mathematician engaged upon a problem. Whether there is a stage at which experience is merely immediate, Bradley says, we have agreed to leave doubtful. But here, I feel sure, he has understated his case, and we may assert positively that there is indeed no such stage. This point is worthy of some elucidation.

On Our Knowledge of Immediate Experience

We are forced, in building up our theory of knowledge, to postulate something given upon which knowledge is founded. And we are forced to a certain extent to consider this construction as something which takes place in time. We think, on the one hand, of material presented to our notice at every moment, and of the whole situation in knowing as a complex with this datum as one of the constituents. And we think also of the development of consciousness in biological evolution as a development of knowledge. And if there is any problem of knowledge at all, neither of these points of view is irrelevant. But we are apt to confuse the two: from the genetic point of view, all of the stages are actualities, whereas the various steps in knowing described in an actual piece of knowing in the mind of an adult man are abstractions, not known as separate objects of attention. They all exist at the same time; there is no priority in our experience of one element or another. When we turn to inspect a lower stage of mind, child or animal, or our own when it is least active, we do not find one or another of these elements into which we analyse the developed consciousness, but we find them all at a lower stage. We do not find feeling without thought, or presentation without reflection: we find both feeling and thought, presentation, redintegration and abstraction, all at a lower stage. And if this is the case, such study of primitive consciousness seems futile; for we find in our own knowing exactly the same constituents, in a clearer and more apprehensible form.

But on the other hand, if all the same constituents were present in every case of knowing, if none were omitted in error, or if none had any temporal precedence over another, all analyses of knowing would be equally tenable. There would be no practical difference: for when there are no bones, anybody can carve a goose. If we did not think that at some moments our consciousness is nearer to 'pure' experience than at others, if we did not think of 'sense-datum' as prior to 'object', if we did not feel that 'act' or 'content', or 'immanent' and 'transcendent' object were not as independent of each other, as capable of entering into different contexts as a table and a chair, the fact of their difference would be a perfect

17

example of useless knowledge. In the philosophy of Bradley we shall find this difficulty in an aggravated form, although a form no more fatal, I think, than the form which it may take in any other philosophy. There is immediate experience, contrasted with ideal construction; which is prior, and in some sense, certainly, prior in time, to the ideal construction. But we go on to find that no actual experience could be merely immediate, for if it were, we should certainly know nothing about it; and also that the line between the experienced, or the given, and the constructed can nowhere be clearly drawn. Then we discover that the difference in no instance holds good outside of a relative and fluctuating point of view. Experience alone is real, but everything can be experienced. And although immediate experience is the foundation and the goal of our knowing, yet no experience is only immediate. There is no absolute point of view from which real and ideal can be finally separated and labelled. All of our terms turn out to be unreal abstractions; but we can defend them, and give them a kind of reality and validity (the only validity which they can possess or can need) by showing that they express the theory of knowledge which is implicit in all our practical activity. And therefore we allow ourselves to hold both that a lower stage of mere feeling is irrelevant and that knowledge is based upon and developed out of feeling.

We may say, then, on turning our attention to lower levels of being, that what we find is not a subtraction, but a general impoverishment. The animal may be as Mr Bradley says 'immersed in practice'; but this is by no means the same thing as immersion in feeling. The animal acts; and any feeling which is acted upon so far goes beyond mere presentation. No stage can be so low as to be mere feeling; and on the other hand man surely feels more than the animal. There is no greater mistake than to think that feeling and thought are exclusive—that those beings which think most and best are not also those capable of the most feeling.

Although there is no stage of life which is more nearly immediate experience than another, and although we are unacquainted with any element in our experience which we can single out as immediate; although we cannot know immediate experience directly as an object, we can yet arrive at it by inference, and even conclude that it is the starting point of our knowing, since it is only in immediate experience that knowledge and its object are one. The fact that we can to a certain extent make an object of it, while at the same time it is not an object among others, not a term which can be in relation to anything else: this throws our explanation into the greatest embarrassment. We are forced to use terms drawn out of it, to handle it as an adjective of either subject or object side, as *my* experience, or as the experienced world. The monistic account is apt to take the first course, pluralism the second. But whether we say 'the world is my experience' or (James, *Essays in Radical Empiricism*, p. 27) that experience 'is made of *that*, of just what appears, of space, of intensity, of flatness, brownness, heaviness, or what not', we have been in either case guilty of importing meanings which hold good only *within* experience. We have no right, except in the most provisional way, to speak of *my* experience, since the I is a construction out of experience, an abstraction from it; and the *thats*, the browns and hards and flats, are equally ideal constructions from experience, as ideal as atoms. An *élan vital* or 'flux' is equally abstracted from experience, for it is only in departing from immediate experience that we are aware of such a process. In short, we can only discuss experience from one side and then from the other, correcting these partial views. This preface is necessary if we are to understand Bradley's use of such terms as 'feeling', 'psychical' or 'spiritual', all of which *seem* to emphasize the subject side of experience.

The real, we are told, is felt. 'To find reality we must betake ourselves to feeling. It is the real, which there appears which is the subject of all predicates.' We must be careful not to identify reality with feeling, either *my* feeling, or collective feeling, or an impersonal current of feeling. Feeling is to be taken (*Appearance*, p. 419) 'as a sort of confusion, and as a nebula which would grow distinct on closer scrutiny'. That of which it is a confusion, and into which it can be analysed, is (*Appearance*, p. 405) 'speaking broadly . . . two great modes, perception and thought on the one side, and will and desire on the other side. Then there is the aesthetic attitude ... and ... pleasure and pain'. Feeling is 'the general state of the total soul not yet at all differentiated into any of the preceding special aspects'. And again it is 'any particular state so far as internally that has undistinguished unity'. Thus immediate experience seems to be in one aspect a condition of the conscious subject. The real appears in feeling, and feeling is 'the general state of the total soul' though we find elsewhere that the soul is itself not real. And even this statement does not tell us that feeling is reality, or even that feeling is real. Feeling is not (*Appearance*, p. 407) a 'consistent aspect of reality' although reality is that which we encounter in feeling or perception.

The reasons for denying that feeling is consistently real are briefly as follows. *Mere* feeling is something which could find no place in a world of objects. It is, in a sense, an abstraction from any actual situation. We have, or seem to have at the start a 'confusion' of feeling, out of which subject and object emerge. We stand before a beautiful painting, and if we are sufficiently carried away, our feeling is a whole which is not, in a sense, *our* feeling, since the painting, which is an object independent of us, is quite as truly a constituent as our consciousness or our soul. The feeling is neither here nor anywhere: the painting is in the room, and my 'feelings' about the picture are in my 'mind'. If this whole of feeling were complete and satisfactory it would not expand into object, and subject with feelings about the object; there would, in fact, be no consciousness. But in order that it should be feeling at all, it must be conscious, but so far as it is conscious it ceases to be merely feeling. Feeling therefore is an aspect, and an inconsistent aspect, in knowing; it is not a separate and isolable phase. On the one hand, feeling is an abstraction from anything actual; on the other hand the objects into which feeling is differentiated have a kind of union which they do not themselves account for; they fuse into each other and stand out upon a background which is merely felt, and from which they are continually requiring supplementation. In order that these developments — thought, will, pleasure and pain, objects — may be possible, feeling must have been given; and when these developments have arrived, feeling has expanded and altered so as to include them. (*Truth and Reality*, p. 175: 'At every moment my state, whatever else it is, is a whole of which I am immediately aware. It is an experienced non-relational unity of many in one.') This is what we mean by saying that feeling is self-transcendent.

Now it is easy to fall into the error of imagining that this self-transcendence of feeling is an event only in the history of souls, and not in the history of the external world. It is hard to disabuse ourselves of the prejudice that feeling is something subjective and private, and that it affects only what feels, not what is felt. The reason for this is not far to seek. Feeling itself is properly speaking neither subjective nor objective, but its development into an articulate whole of terms and relations seems to affect the conscious subject, but not the objects of which the subject is conscious. I have the familiar sensation of red, which develops into a bull in a field; and this may well be an important event to me, affecting my course across the field, without making any impression upon the bull. The only reality which feelings can have, it is thought, is in a consciousness; we do not think of the external world as dependent upon feeling, unless we go so far as to say that it is dependent upon being felt — unless, that is, we think of it as the adjective of some transcendental self. On one side the history of the world is the history of my experience, on the other my experience itself is largely ideal, and requires the existence of much which falls outside of itself. Experience is certainly more real than anything else, but any experience demands reference to something real which lies outside of *that* experience.

We may express the difficulty briefly in this way. In feeling the subject and the object are one. The object becomes an object by its felt continuity with other feelings which fall outside of the finite centre, and the subject becomes a subject by its felt continuity with a core of feeling which is not related to the object. But the point at which a line may be drawn is always a question for partial and practical interests to decide. Everything, from one point of view, is subjective; and everything, from another point of view, is objective; and there is no *absolute* point of view from which a decision may be pronounced. Hence any history of the process must be only relatively true: it must be a history of the object side, postulating the subject, or a history of the subject side, postulating the object side. For feeling, in which the two are one, has no history; it is, as such, outside of time altogether, inasmuch as there is no further point of view from which it can be inspected. In time, there are the two sides, subject and object, neither of which is really stable, independent, the measure of the other. In order to consider how the one came to be as it is, we are forced to attribute an artificial absoluteness to the other. We observe, first, the development of mind in an environment which *ex hypothesi* is not dependent upon mind; and second, in order to conceive the development of the world, in the science of geology, let us say, we have to present it as it would have looked had we, with *our* bodies and our nervous systems, been there to see it. To say that the world really was as we describe it, a million years ago, is a statement which overlooks the development of mind. To say that mind, in its beginnings in child or aborigine or animal, really was as we describe it, is to commit oneself to a relative truth of the same sort. In the same way in our theory of knowledge, when we leave the moment of immediate experience, we are forced to present our account either as the history of mind in its environment, or as the history of the world as it appears to mind.

What I have said is in defence of the use of the word 'feeling'. In describing immediate experience we must use terms which offer a surreptitious suggestion of subject or object. If we say presentation, we think of a subject to which the presentation is present as an object. And if we say feeling, we think of it as the feeling of a subject about an object. And this is only to make of feeling another kind of object, a kind of object which will be discussed in a later chapter. Nevertheless we can arrive at this metaphysical use of the term feeling in its psychological and current use, and show that 'feelings', which are real objects in a world of objects, are different from other objects, are feelings, because of their participation in the nature of feeling in this other sense. The feeling which is an object is feeling shrunk and impoverished, though in a sense expanded and developed as well: shrunk because it is now the object of consciousness, narrower instead of wider than consciousness; expanded because in becoming an object it has developed relations which lead it beyond itself.

Although I speak of 'feelings' as shrunk and impoverished, I do not admit that every feeling was at any stage the whole content of consciousness. The majority of feelings have never succeeded in invading our minds to such an extent as completely to fill it; they have from first to last some objectivity. I do not mean that they are any the less intense for this, or that they disappear under attention. A toothache, or a violent passion, is not necessarily diminished by our knowledge of its causes, its character, its importance or insignificance. To say that one part of the mind suffers and another part reflects upon the suffering is perhaps to talk in fictions. But we know that those highly-organized beings who are able to objectify their passions, and as passive spectators to contemplate their joys and torments, are also those who suffer and enjoy the most keenly. And most of us are able to give a name to some of our feelings, to recognize in a vague way love and hate, envy and admiration, when they arise in our own minds. This naming of feelings, while it may give a very imperfect clue to their nature, is nevertheless of the greatest importance. It is obvious that we can no more explain a passion to a person who has never experienced it than we can explain light to the blind. But it should be obvious also that we can explain the passion equally well: it is no more 'subjective', because some persons have never experienced it, than light is subjective because the blind cannot see. We can explain it by its relations; by its effect upon the heart-beat, its toxic alterations of the system, by its effects in conduct and social intercourse. Without these relations, which give the feeling its whatness, the feeling could not be said to exist. Over and above all relations, it is true, the feeling must be a *that*, merely there; although strictly speaking not anywhere or at any time. But this aspect of mere existence does not distinguish feeling specifically from any other object. No object is exhausted by its relations, and this aspect of mere existence, in all objects as well as feelings, is what we call immediate experience. This aspect of immediacy, of bare existence, is a character of even the most restricted feelings, though they may be at every moment the object of consciousness as well.

We find our feelings, accordingly, on the one side to be of the same nature as immediate experience, and on the other to present no radical difference from other objects. We do not call the furniture of our rooms 'feelings' (unless we mean the mere presence of appearances in our mind) and our ordinary speech declares that two people may share the same feeling as well as regard the same object. Yet we persist in believing that about feelings there is something private, that we cannot 'know' them from the outside; although we are compelled to admit that often an observer understands a feeling better than does the person who experiences it. So far as feelings are objects at all, they exist on the same footing as other objects: they are equally public, they are equally independent of consciousness, they are known and are themselves not knowing. And so far as feelings are merely felt, they are neither subjective nor objective. Let us assume, for the moment, that my experience may consist of one single feeling, and that there is one object before me which I either love or hate. Adhering to my own point of view, in which the feeling is *merely* felt (i.e., I am not conscious of it), the feeling cannot be subjective, for it cannot be said to exist at all. For whom will my feeling be subjective? For the dispassionate observer, who seeing the same object without the same feeling, subtracts my feeling from the object, to make of it a separate and independent entity existing in my mind. In other words, what is subjective is the whole world — the whole world as it is for me — which, because it is (for me) the whole world, cannot be contrasted with anything else 'objective'; and equally truly nothing is subjective. There is no reason, so long as the one feeling lasts and pervades consciousness, why I should cut off part of the total content and call it the object, reserving the rest to myself under the name of feeling. It is only in social behaviour, in the conflict and readjustment of finite centres, that feelings and things are torn apart. And after this separation they leave dim and drifting edges, and tend to coalesce.

We must maintain, then, that in any cognition there is never more than a practical separation between the object and that which apprehends it. The object stands out, if you will, against a background of experience; and although it has relations which fall outside of our experience, it is likewise an abstraction from experience, continually capable of subtraction or addition. 'The object before me is unstable and it moves so as to satisfy me . . . I insist that in addition to other influences (whose working I admit), the object is moved also by that which is merely felt. There are connections of content now actually present in feeling, and these are able to jar with the object before me. And they are able further to correct that object by supplementation from themselves.'[2]

With the status of the feeling become objective I shall be occupied in a later chapter; it is here only necessary to insist on the validity of the continuous transition by which feeling becomes object and object becomes feeling. One important case of this transition is sense-deception. The resolution of contradictions of sense may be found in a process of assimilation of feeling to a new object, or in assimilation of object to feeling. In the case of the stick in water, for example, the real object for the psychologist may include not only the 'real' stick but an instance of refraction. That the object in the illusion is quite as real as the 'real' object is a truth to which the new realism has well called attention. The new object and the false, we may add, are continuous, and the new object has been constructed by adding to the old object elements which were first experienced and not contemplated.

We are not here concerned with the absolute objective criterion for the permanence and independence of any special class of objects; it is enough if we can make clear that we have no immediate distinction between object and feeling. It may accordingly be said that the real situation is an experience which can never be wholly defined as an object nor wholly enjoyed as a feeling, but in which any of the observed constituents may take on the one or the other aspect. The further question is this: to what extent can we say that identity persists in such a change: to what extent may we say that the felt feeling and the observed feeling are the *same*? With the general question of identity we are not here concerned. But between the special case of identity of which I speak and identity in the usual sense there is a striking difference. The latter is identity of objects (points of attention). This case is not the identity of two feelings both objectified. It is the identity of something which is an object with something which is not. When the difference is noted the very statement of the question will I think provide the answer. There is, between the felt and the objectified feeling, a continuity which is not interrupted by any objective difference; and so far as there is no perceived difference we may assume the two to be the same.

This rather subtle question, which really belongs to a later part of the discussion, is worth some little detail here. In considering how far feeling may be an object (and may be known) we may ask whether our conclusions will have a bearing upon experimental psychology. We may say that if psychology sets up a sharp factual line of demarcation between processes and things, and yet proposes to investigate the former as objects of science, it is committed to a contradiction.* Introspection can give us only terms, and not processes. In the same way as the mathematical representation of motion is and is not the same as the motion represented, so the object in psychology is and is not the same as the process. And it is only when psychology pretends to deal with something more 'subjective' or more philosophic than the subject-matter of any other science that its pretensions lead it astray.

Yet to say that we have no knowledge of the process, of feeling and the transition from the merely felt to the objectified would be even more a vagary. The transition is not saltatory. It is neither wholly unconscious nor capricious, but is more or less a willed change. The attention to the feeling presupposes that there is such an object present, and that the attention has not manufactured the object (*Truth and Reality*, pp. 162 ff.). So that in

* See Joachim, *Mind* 69, January 1909, and G. E. Moore and Dawes Hicks in *Proc. Arist. Soc.*, 1909–10, on the subject-matter of psychology.

attending to a sensation or feeling any change of which we are aware besides the change felt in attending may be attributed to the sensation or feeling and held to be independent of the attention; and if we are aware of no other change than the attention, we may consider that any other change is meaningless.

The more fundamental aspect of the question, however, is this (*Truth and Reality*, p. 169): 'In any emotion one part of that emotion consists already of objects, of perceptions and ideas before my mind. And, the whole emotion being one, the special group of feeling is united with these objects before my mind, united with them integrally and directly though not objectively. . . . For when the object-part of our emotion is enlarged by further perception or idea, the agreement or disagreement with what is felt is not merely general and suffused, but is located through the object in one special felt group. And this special connexion and continuity with the object explains, I think, how we are able further to transform what is observed by the addition of elements from what is felt. There are features in feeling (this is the point) which already in a sense belong to and are one with their object, since the emotion contains and unites both its aspects.'

The error, then, would consist in any sharp division between enjoyment and contemplation, either in general or at any particular moment, or in treating the distinction of feeling and object as a possible *scientific* distinction. Science may make the distinction between feeling of object and object of feeling, but it cannot make a distinction between feeling and object as such. And now we are in a better position to inquire into the situation (in order not to say relation) of feeling, thought and object in experience. It will be recognized, first, that experience is non-relational. Relations can hold only between terms, and these terms can exist only against the background of an experience which is not itself a term. The objectified feeling of psychology does not exist apart from the rest of feeling which is merely felt, no matter how negligible that rest of feeling may appear. But within experience we always find relations, and in this sense we may say that non-relational experience does not exist. These relations, however, are not experience, and while they are experienced and therefore real, they are not real as relations. Yet, just as relations, they seem to be essential to reality. In this way a contradiction has 'broken out'. 'Feeling has a content, and this content is not consistent within itself. . . .'³ This situation it is which prompts us to pass on by new construction to a larger felt whole in which the same puzzling terms and relations appear. No experience is self-consistent, because of the ideal aspects with which it is shot through. Yet these ideal aspects are likewise real, and themselves issue from a felt background.

We may now go on to consider the place of consciousness in experience. In order to understand Bradley's answer to this problem we must keep in mind two different and apparently contradictory aspects of the situation. Experience, we have been told, is not co-extensive with consciousness, but is wider. 'There is an immediate feeling, a knowing and being in one, with which knowledge begins' (*Truth and Reality*, p. 159). Feeling is more than either object or subject, since in a way it includes both. On the other hand, we must remember that the conscious subject, as a construction, falls partly outside of any whole of feeling. 'The finite content is necessarily determined from the outside.'⁴ We must therefore expect to find consciousness to be both something immediately given and something which would not be in the immediate experience unless it also extended beyond it. Consciousness is not an entity, but an aspect, and an inconsistent aspect, of reality. Experience, we may assert, both begins and ends in something which is not conscious. And that this 'not conscious' is not what we call 'unconscious' should be sufficiently obvious. For what we term unconscious is simply an element *in* experience which arises in *contrast* to other elements in experience. It refers either to certain supposed mental entities which guide or influence our conscious actions. And I need not point out that this use of the term is of very doubtful value. Undoubtedly our mental life is directed by many influences of which we are not conscious, and undoubtedly there is no clear line to be drawn between that of which we are conscious and that which as 'feeling'

melts imperceptibly into a physiological background. But so far
as this fringe is contrasted with that which is actually conscious,
it is merely an object in our world like any other. And the 'unconscious' conceived merely as external objects is only the un-
feeling; it is the other side of experience and not the whole. The
unconscious, in short, denotes something within experience, as
the conscious does, and neither of these terms will represent the
whole.

At the beginning then consciousness and its object are one. So
far we are in agreement with at least two schools of contemporary
philosophy.* We can say with James (*Radical Empiricism*, p. 23)
'the instant field of the present is . . . only virtually or potentially
either subject or object'. Confining ourselves to this instant field
(which we must remember is only an abstraction) we grant that
no division can be found between an awareness and that of which
it is aware. We cannot allow Mr Russell's supposition of a 'consciousness' which might merely exist for a moment and experience
a sensation of red. The 'red' would simply be a 'neutral entity'
which might be taken as mental or physical according to context,
but where there is no context there is neither mental nor physical.
What James calls the context is that of which Bradley speaks when
he says that the finite content is 'determined from the outside'.
This determination from the outside is unending. In the first
place, there is my present physical constitution, which determines
the experience without being an element in it, and there is my
whole past, conceived either as the history of my body or as the
sequence of my conscious experiences, so far as I can detach them
from the objects in the experience, and consider them only as
adjectives of myself. And secondly, there are the nature and the
connections of the object, which fall outside of the present moment
of experience, and are discovered on closer scrutiny. As we develop
subject and object side, they seem to approximate independence,
for the object is certainly independent of this knower, and the
knower independent of any particular object: on the one side we
get souls or selves, on the other the physical universe. That

* And in opposition to Russell and Moore.

objects are dependent upon consciousness, or consciousness upon objects, we most resolutely deny. Consciousness, we shall find, is reducible to relations between objects, and objects we shall find to be reducible to relations between different states of consciousness; and neither point of view is more nearly ultimate than the other. But if we attempt to put the world together again, after having divided it into consciousness and objects, we are condemned to failure. We cannot create experience out of entities which are independent of experience. Nor could we be conscious at all unless these ideal connections somehow entered into the experience, breaking up its immediate unity. Yet the original unity — the 'neutral entity' — though transcended, remains, and is never analysed away. In our perception of the red flower the original mere red, in which awareness and awared are one, persists.

We can assert much more than seems implied in the last sentence. It is not merely 'in my experience' that the moment of identity is essential. My existence is dependent upon my experience of red in the flower, and the existence of the flower is dependent upon its unity in feeling (as red) with me. Whatever relations the flower may afterwards be discovered to have, its nature must be such that its being under these conditions experienced as red will be essential to the whole account of it. The real flower, we can say, will be the sum of its effects — its actual effects upon other entities — and this sum must form a system, must somehow hang together. And if we attribute to the flower any other reality besides these effects, which are actual only in experiences, we are thrown back upon what it is for itself — i.e., upon its experience of itself. And here we only face the old difficulties of subject and object over again in the form of pan-psychism. To carry the problem to this point may be possible. Neither attacking nor defending the pan-psychist view, I consider it negligible. For if the existence of subject or object is always relative, then the point to which we elaborate this relativity is a matter of indifference.

Thus we are led to the conclusion that the only independent reality is immediate experience or feeling. And we have seen that to think of feeling as subjective, as the mere adjective of a subject, is only a common prejudice. So far as it is feeling and nothing more, it is self-sufficient and demands no further supplementation. 'My' feeling is certainly in a sense mine. But this is because and in so far as I *am* the feeling. I do not in consequence know (in the sense of understand) my own feeling better than does an outsider. If it be objected that I must have a feeling in order to understand it, the same may be said of every other object in the world.

Immediate experience, we have seen, is a timeless unity which is not as such present either any*where* or to any*one*. It is only in the world of objects that we have time and space and selves. By the failure of any experience to be merely immediate, by its lack of harmony and cohesion, we find ourselves as conscious souls in a world of objects. We are led to the conception of an all-inclusive experience outside of which nothing shall fall. If anyone object that mere experience at the beginning and complete experience at the end are hypothetical limits, I can say not a word in refutation for this would be just the reverse side of what opinions I hold. And if anyone assert that immediate experience, at either the beginning or end of our journey, is annihilation and utter night, I cordially agree. That Mr Bradley himself would accept this interpretation of his (*Truth and Reality*, p. 188) 'positive non-distinguished non-relational whole' is not to be presumed. But the ultimate nature of the Absolute does not come within the scope of the present paper. It is with some of the intermediate steps that the following chapters are concerned.

CHAPTER II

On the Distinction of
'Real' and 'Ideal'

The conclusion of the preceding chapter has been that reality as we may know it, the ultimate criterion which gives meaning to our judgments of existence, is so far as it appears at all, our experience, yet an experience which only to a certain extent — from a certain necessary but untenable point of view—is 'ours'. As a development and in support of this conclusion, we are driven to question the status of those elements within experience which exist only by virtue of their reference to other elements which are, in that reference, real, and we shall come to the conclusion that the apparently fundamental separation between the real and the ideal is but tentative and provisional, a moment in a process. This conclusion is nothing new; it is no novelty even in the essay which I shall chiefly quote, that on 'Floating Ideas and the Imaginary'* (*Mind*, October 1906); it is familiar to students of Hegel. I can only plead that I seem to find it constantly neglected or misinterpreted. Accordingly, after a general statement of the theory, I shall attempt to make the position clearer by criticism of such systems as would do without this theory, and shall try to show its full importance in the thought of Mr Bradley. Afterwards I shall attempt to point out some un-developed consequences for the theory of objects, in regard to unreal and imaginary objects, 'intended' objects, and process (act) as object. The whole discussion, needless to say, is bound up very closely with that of perception and judgment, which will immediately follow.

* Reprinted in *Truth and Reality*.

On the Distinction of 'Real' and 'Ideal'

The theory, in its general terms, is stated in *Appearance*, Chapter XXIV. 'There is a view which takes, or attempts to take, sense-perception as the one known reality. And there is a view which endeavours, on the other side, to consider appearance in time as something indifferent. . . . We have seen that the separation of the real into idea and existence is a division admissible only within the world of appearance. . . . In order to be fact at all, each presentation must exhibit ideality. . . . But the union in all perception of thought with sense, the co-presence everywhere in all appearances of fact with ideality — this is the one foundation of truth.' And further, 'when an idea qualifies the universe, how can it be excluded from reality?' (*Appearance*, pp. 334–5.)

The ordinary view of the relation of real and ideal I take to be this. We are given in 'experience' something called fact which is real because independent, and independent because real. This fact is not necessarily fact of sense perception, or of physical reality, but the fact may be itself an idea from an external point of view, an idea placed in reality. And the objection that a fact is always an objective, and not simply a *that*, does not in the popular view militate against its independence. The fact may appear with its fullest development of definition, with innumerable stipulations of relationship, yet we 'apprehend' it as independent, and proceed to erect between it and its percipient an abstraction called thought, the existence of which is its reference to reality. And popular epistemology then asks us to accept the elaborated and sophisticated object as 'real', and yet to maintain the proviso that all the positive qualifications which make it just what it is are products of the 'activity of thought'. In other words, the popular theory of knowledge, from which our philosophies spring, is realistic and nominalistic at the same time. That this is a just description I think there will be little question; and whatever direction our solutions take, I doubt whether we ever wholly escape the crude antithesis.

Now there are several ways in which this difficulty is escaped or evaded. The simplest is that of sensation and thought, or, as in the Kantian philosophy, the distinction between an external reality from which we receive material, and the formative activity of consciousness. This distinction — ultimately that between activity and passivity — will serve to classify a vast number of systems, both idealistic and realistic; for I am not satisfied merely that the distinction should be finally transcended, but wish to enquire into its validity as a starting point. So that a conational psychology such as that of Mr Alexander, or of Lipps — any psychology which deals with 'processes' as its subject-matter — will fall into a class with such an idealism as was recently advocated by Professor Adams.* And the second attitude is that of psychologists such as Stout, who would make a sharp distinction between content and object, and between psychical and physical object.** This I believe is the more usual attitude in psychology. And again there is the view of those who would reduce everything to object and immediate apprehension, reducing the 'activity' of thought to a minimum, as Meinong, Russell, or Miss Wodehouse.

These views it will be necessary to criticize, but without some elaboration of the point of view from which these criticisms will be made, what I have to say may appear inconsequent and negative. The common complaint, accordingly, lodged against all these views, is that it does not matter from what point of view or with what data you start, you will, if you do not stop arbitrarily, come to one conclusion; and whether or no psychology has the right to stop, whether psychology is independent of metaphysics, will be one of the questions involved. And, according to this view, activity and passivity, immediacy and mediation, acquaintance and description, will be transcended in the process of completion of our knowledge. In the words of Mr Bosanquet:*** 'we shall . . . meet, with uncompromising resistance, the attempt to take any form of immediateness, understood as excluding mediation, for an absolute and reliable datum, whether in the form of an object of simple apprehension, called by the name of fact, or in the form of an indeterminate creative impulse called by the name of life, or in

* *Philos. Rev.*, 1913.
** See his controversy with Mr Joseph.
*** *Prin. of Indiv. and Value*, p. 13.

the form of a subject of experience, impervious and isolated, called by the name of "self"'.

The first point to be made is that the difference between real and ideal is in a sense an ideal difference. It is created within a limited sphere of meaning and recognizable only within that sphere. If we would recognize a difference between reality and its attributes, we must have become aware of the fact of error, and of alterations of content in relation to the same intended object. We become aware that we have intended a reality, that we have, within our experience, delimited a field as real; that we have brought this field into relation with ourselves: and in error and in alterations of content we come to consider meaning as another reality beside that which it intends. This discovery must be qualified in two ways. First, the reality which we have intended is an ideal construction. It is not reality as a whole, but the radiation from a particular and indefinable point; a field of quite uncertain extent, assumed and selected. And second, the idea with which this reality is qualified is itself real, though of a reality which we cannot possibly define; for, though its existence as a fact is another thing from its meaning, yet its meaning is inextricably involved in its existence as a fact. The idea is something real, or it could not be even ideal; and on the other hand the reality to which it refers is an ideal reality, cut off, in a sense, and isolated; for the attribution of an idea to reality as such is not within our power. On the other hand, the reality intended tends to identify itself with the content of the idea; and on the other hand this content pretends to identify itself with reality. Without the ideal aspect of the real the distinction would be impossible. And unless the idea were itself real it would be unable to relate itself to reality.

But how, it will be said, will these statements be reconciled with the previous assertions that reality is experience? You have first defined reality as experience, and have then declared experience to be indefinable: you now pretend that we have always before us an ideal fragment which we call reality, and of which we predicate the ideal. Are not the two statements hopelessly at variance? If the

35

first statement about reality is true, how can the second reality be real in any sense; and have we not rather a wholly imaginary world of imaginary predications completely cut off, as far as our knowledge and acquaintance goes, from the reality upon which you have insisted?

In order to reply to this objection, in which the whole realistic position is implied, it will be necessary to dispose of a difficult prejudice. The real and the ideal (including the unreal) are not two separate groups of objects. Nor, as we shall see, can they be distinguished as object and 'process' or 'act'. Neither the absolute real nor the absolute ideal can as such enter into discourse; it is only when two entities 'take of each other', so to speak, that either of them can be real or ideal. Reality is simply that which is intended and the ideal is that which intends; and ultimately — for we have no reason to stop — the intending is the totality of intending, and the intended is the whole of reality. This whole of reality, of course, will as discussed present both real and ideal aspects; but this differentiation in what should be simple will fall outside of our metaphysics (*Appearance*, p. 352). It is inclusive with reference to our system, and that is all that we require.*

The division of real and ideal into two groups of objects is an action of a natural and inevitable tendency. As we shall later urge, an object is simply that to which we attend, and we cannot attend to process or idea without making it to that extent an object. But, just as no object is wholly object, so we can, by constant correction and discretion, to some degree handle idea without reducing it wholly to object. In the first place, we must remember that the distinction of real and ideal is one that does not arise until the ideal is recognized as having a reality of its own, apart (in a sense) from its meaning; and yet as preserving its identity in this new aspect. Without the '*Mitmensch*' (fellow man) and our introjection the question of ideality would never arise. It is easy to mistake the issue here, and to say that the idea is simply not recognized. We

---

* 'Wherever the idea can be merely *one aspect* [italics mine] of a single presentation, there we can say that the ideal content exists, and is an actual event.' *Appearance*, p. 352.

can imagine a solitary autochthon, yet gifted with reason and, if you like, with some power of expression, making judgments, quite unaware of their ideal relation to the reality intended. And for this hermit, as a centre of experience, these judgments will simply not come into question — the question as to their existence will be one to which there is no answer, either affirmative or negative. And this is everywhere the case, that until the ideal is recognized as real, it is not even ideal. And I use the word 'recognize' with this in view: the idea as idea (as meaning) is neither existent nor non-existent, and could we consistently keep to this internal view it would not be real. It will be said, I know, that the externality of the idea is implied in its internality. But this implication exists only for a point of view which contains both points of view.

With these considerations in mind, let us return to the discussion of the relation of Reality as subject, to reality as the fragment to which predicates are assigned.* In any case of judgment or perception something is assumed to be real, and this something is a background of indefinite extent continuous with the content which is asserted of it. The background has ideal characteristics which are rather felt than predicated, and which are capable of indefinite transmutation in a more and more inclusive view. This provisional reality has, on the one hand, the character of an ideal construction, for it is a sphere in which our ideal activity has been exercising itself; and on the other hand it is apart from the particular idea at the moment and under the aspect of predication. It is, in contrast with that idea, *accepted*; and the ideal aspect of it is for the occasion negligible, in contrast with the particular idea with which we are engaged. Thus, of course, an idea may justly be predicated of an ideal world; and our interpretation of the character of Ivanhoe may qualify the assumed reality of the story just as truly as the story itself, as a story, qualifies reality. The ideal world of the story qualifies reality — in what way, we are ultimately in ignorance — and

* 'It would be impossible that any man should have a world, the various provinces of which were quite rationally connected, or appeared always in system.... He means, from time to time, by reality some one region of the Real, which habitually he fails to distinguish and define.' *Appearance*, p. 325.

through this world our conception of the character of Ivanhoe is attached to reality. The question of imaginary and unreal objects belongs to a later part of the discussion. There is however one objection likely to be raised at this point, related to that question. The objection is this: the assertion that reality is always the subject is in apparent conflict with the fact of judgments in which reality is a predicate. In the judgment 'X is real' is reality the subject? The answer is this: In this judgment the subject is not a presentation which we call real or leave in the void. It is already largely placed and determined. It is already predicated of a world which has two spheres, and the question is: through which of the two it shall be related to the whole. The titular subject is already real, and the adjectival reality is only the assertion of one sphere in which it belongs. Yet in the course of the assertion the nature of the subject has altered. If the reality which we assert is the reality of ghosts, then the ghost as potential subject, previous to the judgment, is not the same ghost as that with which we emerge. The latter is a real ghost; and how can we say that the content of a real ghost is not different from that of an imagined or merely presented ghost? The subject, then, cannot have been the ghost, and the predicate cannot have been reality; for, on the one hand, the subject of a judgment cannot be altered by the judgment, and on the other hand, the predicate must add something to our knowledge — and we knew already that the ghost was in some sense real.

With the connection between the predication inside the proposition and the predication referring to the subject outside the judgment I shall be concerned later. I must call attention here, however, to the fact that the idea which is predicated of reality is not the content of a single word. The statement that ghosts are real is not, as we have seen, the predicating ghosts of reality. An idea is never given in a single word ('only in the sentence does the word first acquire actual life and being'*) when that word is an element in a judgment and not in itself the expression of a judgment.

* See Jerusalem, *Urteilsfunction*, p. 28: 'Das Wort, . . . gewinne erst im Satze wirkliches Leben und Sein. . . .' and *passim*, for relation of word to idea.

On the Distinction of 'Real' and 'Ideal'

The fact that words are always used in the expression of ideas, and are remembered and placed by attachment to a more or less indefinite group of ideas in which they have been used, may lead us to regard ideas as the meaning of words. Now there is a decided difference. ('The isolated substantive name lacks the positing therein of a subject, and hence it cannot be presented here, at the locus of perception, as a living source of multifarious activity. . . . It will be seen that the meanings of isolated words must be so presented, as if nothing in perception corresponded to them; they are founded purely on the articulate sounds we make, and in this alone possess a basis for their existence.'*) A word, it is true, may mean or stand for, an idea. But there will never obtain an identity between the meaning of the word as concept, and the meaning of the word as idea. As an idea it is predicated of reality, assigned a place in a system — more or less complete — which is assumed as real. But the concept — greenness, or triangularity — does not as such qualify reality at all. It is, in itself, neither real nor unreal. The meaning of a concept always exceeds the idea, and is of virtually indefinite extension. When we predicate the reality of ghosts, for example, we qualify reality, an ideal reality abstracted from the whole, by the idea of *real* ghosts; and this idea includes, on one side, much more than the word or concept ghost. The ghost conceived as real is a special kind of content with characteristics continuous with those of the fragment of reality in which he is set; the idea, from one point of view apart from the world and attached to it, yet contains already the character of the world, a world, as I said before, which shows by the very fact that that idea can be attached to it that it is somehow prepared for the reception of that idea.

In this way I make the distinction between concept and idea.

---

* Gerber, *Sprache u. Erkennen*, pp. 102-3, is clear as to the unpresentability (*Unvorstellbarkeit*) of the word: 'Es fehlt dem isolierten nomen substantivum dies, dass in ihm ein Subjekt gesetzt ist, und so kann es nicht hier, an dem wahrgenommenen Orte vorgestellt werden als lebendige Quelle mehrfacher Thätigkeit, . . . Man sieht, dass die Bedeutungen der isolierten Worter so vorgestellt werden müssen, wie ihnen in der Wahrnehmung nichts entspricht; sie gründen sich lediglich auf unsere Sprachlaute und haben nur an diesen den Boden für ihr Dasein.'— I fail to find, however, a clear distinction between concept and idea on the one hand, and idea and image on the other.

On the Distinction of 'Real' and 'Ideal'

The idea is the total content which we mean about reality in any particular presentation. It is not purely or even primarily psychological, for its meaning is essential (and meaning, as I shall have occasion to consider later, does not as such form an object for psychology); and furthermore, its meaning partially coincides with the reality which it intends. Nor is the idea purely a logical entity, since it always, in the end, comes to occupy a particular place in a real world. The concept, on the other hand, while it may in a sense — loosely, as I think — be called ideal, is not to be confounded with the ideality of the idea, and indeed in contrast with the idea had much better be called real.* The concept, in the first place, is extra-mental; it exceeds all actual and possible content, or definition. Nothing can secure you against the possibility that new experience may add to the meaning by extending the use. And properly speaking, a concept cannot be defined at all, for to define it is to restrict it to a definite circle of ideas. So far as it is thus identified with these ideas it ceases to be a concept; so far as it is present and practical, it is used to stand for a (not wholly definite) group of ideas. In this way we come mistakenly to identify the concept with one or several of its related ideas — to consider it as appearance as well as reality. And it is true that reality exists only through its appearances. It is only in some sense in ideas that concepts exist; and, in a sense, the pointing of the ideas at the concept constitutes the reality of the concept; its reality consists of the self-transcendence of ideas.

I am not confident that these definitions are valid ones, but they attempt to avoid Bradley's confusion of concepts with ideas, and Moore's confusion of ideas with concepts. Moore's criticisms of the passages in Bradley have however a certain force. 'Now to Mr

* Professor Hoernle ('Image, Idea, and Meaning,' p. 90) makes the following distinction between the real and the ideal: '1. In the first place, the contrast between idea and reality is taken to be a contrast between present reality and something which in some sense or another is "not present". Thus the past and the future are usually said to be "ideal" as against the reality of present experience; and again in volition we have the opposition between my present state and an idea of change, the "realization" of which would satisfy me. 2. Secondly, reality as contrasted with idea, is more particularly identified with sense perception.' — But I do not find this classification adequate; and it makes no place for the concept.

On the Distinction of 'Real' and 'Ideal'

Bradley's argument that "the idea in judgment is the universal meaning" I have nothing to add.' But he says further, 'I shall in future use the term "concept" for what Mr Bradley calls a "universal meaning"; since the term "idea" is plainly full of ambiguities, whereas "concept" and its German equivalent *Begriff* have been more nearly appropriated to the use in question.' This concept he substitutes for idea in such a use as the following: '... that the "idea used in judgment" is not a part of the content of our ideas, nor produced by any action of our minds, and that hence truth and falsehood are not dependent on the relation of *our* ideas to reality' where the idea used in judgment is properly an idea and not a concept.[5] Both Bradley and Moore make but one distinction — that between a *psychical* idea and a *logical* idea. Russell (*Problems*, p. 99) makes a similar distinction: in 'the sense in which it denotes the *object* of an act of thought, whiteness is an "idea". Hence, if the ambiguity is not guarded against, we may come to think that whiteness is an "Idea" in the other sense, *i.e.* an act of thought; and thus we come to think that whiteness is mental.'

Bosanquet (*Essentials*, p. 74) hardly differs: ' "Idea" has two principal meanings. (*a*) A psychical presentation and (*b*) An identical reference.'

It should be immediately evident that the idea in Bradley's judgment is a very different thing from the concept in Moore's. We do not in judgment, certainly, simply predicate of reality the content, or part of the content, of a so-called 'mental state'. So far we are all in accord. In 'Caesar crossed the Rubicon' the idea is just as 'external' as the reality of which it is predicated. But the idea in question is not a concept, but something of indefinite complexity. Caesar's crossing the Rubicon (the objective) has, as we consider it, elements which attach it more and more in one way or another to the real. The movement is not simply the movement of an idea toward reality; but the real comes to join itself, by presenting ideal aspects which are also real, to the self-realizing idea. The idea was never at any moment of the process detached and 'floating'. In being an idea at all, it must mean to be real; it is

41

no more mental than the reality to which it is attached; its ideality consists in its meaning, and cannot be considered as a quality or mark by which it may be distinguished from the real. Hence, in the judgment above instanced the idea is the whole reality meant — and I shall try to show later, the whole meaning is ultimately the whole of reality.

It is at once apparent that neither of the definitions used by Bosanquet is adequate for idea in this sense. This is rather what idealists are accustomed to call 'ideal content'. Content is as equivocal a word as any, but I cannot see that any distinction is introduced by using 'ideal content' instead of idea. The idea predicated of reality is not part of any 'content'* nor is it composed of simpler ideas. It is meaningless, I think, to speak of the 'content' of the idea: is the content anything but the idea itself? for so far as the content is discrepant with the idea, I cannot see that it is the content of *that* idea.

There are here several issues:

1. the relation of idea to mental content
2. the relation of idea to image
3. the relation of idea to concept and speech
4. the relation of idea to identical reference

Let us consider the last question first. I wish to distinguish idea from 3 and from 4, and 3 and 4 from each other. Fixed reference is thus manipulated by Bosanquet (*Logic*, I, p. 69): '... the idea, as used in judgment, is a general signification, or in other words, a fixed reference. And because fixed, it is limited; limited to portions of content which serve as indices of the reference, and are compatible with psychical accompaniments that vary with the series of images.'

The essence of an idea, for Bosanquet, seems to be that it should refer to something (*Essentials*, p. 75: the identity which two people mean to mean when they say 'Saint Paul's Cathedral' is the idea). What, in this case, is the idea? It is hardly the actual

---

* Bosanquet, *Logic*, I, p. 44; 'I ... shall follow Mr Bradley in using "idea" for a fixed content or logical meaning, not for the psychical images which pass through the mind and never recur. ...'

object meant — the object is that to which the idea refers. It is not the word or sound 'Cathedral', nor is it the intention of the two people to refer to the same thing; it is the fact of their reference to the same thing. And '. . . the content of this reference *is* the object of our thought'.[6] Now the idea, in this sense, can hardly be the idea which is predicated of reality. It is (*Essentials*, pp. 78–9) a 'concrete habit or tendency', a 'selective rule', and again it is a thing ('mental unit or image') which stands for something else.*

The idea predicated of reality cannot be either a 'mental presentation' or a conation, nor can it be simply a meaning — for a meaning always means to be something more than a meaning. It is not certainly a compound of simpler elements. Bradley is clear on this point (*Logic*, p. 12): 'We may say . . . that all (judgments) have but one (idea). We take an ideal content, a complex totality of qualities and relations, and we then introduce divisions and distinctions, and we call these products separate ideas with relations between them. And this is quite unobjectionable. But what is objectionable, is our then proceeding to deny that the whole before our mind is a single idea. . . . The relations between the ideas are themselves ideal. . . . And the whole in which they subsist is ideal, and so one idea'. There is here a fixed reference in the sense that the idea aims to be (though any expression one can use will remain a metaphor) a reality, and the latter, as real, is independent of its relations. The fixity of the reference is not the character of fixity of meaning which the words have in language, nor is its fixity due to a composition of these fixities. It is not as if I took a number of sentence elements which have each an identity of reference and compounded them into a whole which has an identity by virtue of the ingredient identities. The idea, though largely dependent for its existence upon the forms of its expression, must yet not be confused with these forms. The idea is that reality which I intend, and the identity is only the

* Mr Bosanquet says (*Essentials*, p. 79) 'Mere mental facts, occurrences in my mental history, taken as such, cannot enter into judgment'. But I should ask whether the so-called mental facts are mental at all, and whether they do not enter into judgment just as do any other 'non-mental' facts.

assumption of *one* world; it is not the characteristic of it as idea, but as world.

The idea, and its predication of reality, may exist previous to the articulation of language. It is not true that language is simply a development of our ideas; it is a development of reality as well. The idea is developed from within, as language shows a richness of content and intricacy of connections which it assumes to have been really there, but which are as well an enrichment of the reality grasped. Wherever there is an appreciation of a presentation and a relating of it to the subject's world there is an idea and a judgment: and this is practically universal. The sea-anemone which accepts or rejects a proffered morsel is thereby relating an idea to the sea-anemone's world. The fixity is simply this reference to a definite place in the world — a world which is built up from the subject's point of view. This, for the subject, is the only world, but it is not a solipsistic world, for it is not contrasted with any other possible world.

These remarks have been directed against such an interpretation of Bosanquet's definition as would infer that the idea, as idea, detached from its reality, need mean the same thing for various subjects. 'Saint Paul's' might retain its full fixity of meaning for me if everyone else meant by the same term, let us say 'Notre-Dame'. There would, of course, be contradiction in my world which I should have to rectify in one way or another; but the social consilience goes toward the construction of our world and not toward the definition of idea.

It is in this sense, then, that idea involves identical reference. The inquiry brings us consequently to the relation of idea to its articulated content and to the concept. The idea in predication is not necessarily of definite extent; it may be extended or narrowed or analysed. We are familiar with the objection 'but you imply much more than this' — or 'but you mean no more than — ' and sometimes are immediately aware of an expansion or contraction of our idea. And again the idea may be analysed into component ideas. In the example which Bradley has given (*Logic*, pp. 12–13) we may first have an idea *wolf-eating-lamb*, and from this we separate the ideas, let us say, of *wolf*, of *lamb*, and perhaps further, of *eating*. And this fact would at first seem to controvert what I have said, above (p. 38), for we seem to have an idea for each word. I should reiterate the distinction between word as concept and word as idea. There may be, in a sense, degrees of ideality and conceptuality. In all judgment, even of the simplest sort, there is involved recognition. The actual idea judged, it is true, is unique, or the judgment would not be made, but the judgment is made only through universal connections. In the cruder perception, *wolf-eating-lamb*, these connections are few and indistinct; in the developed knowledge we notice elements in this one idea which can be isolated through their relation to elements in other judgments, and which attain the status of ideas by bringing these relations with them to the particular case, so that the result is that a complex of connections is present in the particular perception or judgment, and besides being evoked by the idea, tends itself to become an idea and be judged about. And for this idea the one word (*wolf*, if you like) may stand. Yet it is a mutilation of connections to say that the one word stands for this 'idea'. For it does so only by virtue of its close connection with a number of more primary ideas. The *wolf* has become a reality perceived or judged, on a higher plane, as *wolf-eating-lamb* was in cruder knowledge; and this evolution of the idea can go on to the degree of abstraction upon which we find it practicable to live. This, then, is an idea 'of higher order', composed out of lower ideas and capable of entering as an ingredient in more particular ideas which are predicated of reality. The ideas of higher order are themselves less frequently predicated, for obvious reasons; their existence usually implies their assumption as ideal elements of reality (*Kraftcentra*). And these ideas of higher order, in their turn upon a higher plane, may be elements, rather felt than judged, in judgments of higher order, which in their own way are like the primitive judgments attributing a total situation to reality.*

* These levels of idea and judgment correspond, of course, to tne levels of experience referred to in the essay of Bradley, used above ('On Our Knowledge of Immediate Experience').

On the Distinction of 'Real' and 'Ideal'

We have marked briefly the steps in the development of general ideas. And we find that the generality of an idea is a matter of degree; every perception involves some degree of recognition and the operation of a universal. Accordingly we must now ask, what is the difference between such a general idea and a concept? I define concept (see pp. 39–40) as that which a word denotes, and idea (or general idea) as that to which a word refers in reality, this reference being contingent. And a concept, as I have said (p. 40) is a thing-in-itself; it can be suggested, rather than defined, through more and more general ideas, but is at no point to be identified with these ideas. The concept it is of which the word is properly the sign or symbol. I am in partial agreement with Sigwart (I, p. 42): 'Words are generally held to be signs of Concepts. But a Concept in the logical sense is a work of art, produced by a conscious elaboration of our ideas in which its characteristics are analysed and its definition fixed, and it is the work of logic to help us to attain to the ideal state in which words represent such Concepts.' Of course I should be unwilling to admit that a concept is a 'work of art' or that it is in any way *created* by thought, or that greenness, triangularity, or to the right of, is '*produced by* a conscious elaboration of our ideas'. There is no meaning, so far as I can see, in saying either that the concept is created or that it is 'eternal'. In a sense, concepts are omnipresent, and in a sense, they are never known at all. We have, in the simplest case in which a concept appears, an intuitive knowledge of it (if one likes to talk of intuition), and on the other hand as I say, beyond intuitive 'knowledge' we know the concept only through ideas — through its appearances. And we must not confuse the development of the language with development in concepts; for it would, I think, be more apt to say that the development of language is the history of our exploration of the world of concepts. The goal of language is in this sense unattainable, for it is simply that of a complete vocabulary of concepts, each independent of the rest; and all of which, by their various combinations, would give complete and final knowledge — which would, of course, be knowledge without a knower.

46

If this be true, how are we to estimate Mr Moore's assertion that 'a proposition is composed of concepts'? He accepts Bradley's statement that the idea in judgment is the universal meaning; but we have interpreted this universal meaning and Bosanquet's 'fixed' or 'identical' reference as an ideal reality in the form of universal connections; and not as the concept. Mr Moore postulates the ultimate vocabulary of which I have spoken. Once given this vocabulary of concepts, it would be quite true to say, as Moore does say (*Mind* 1899, p. 182), 'the world is formed of concepts. These are the only objects of knowledge. A thing becomes intelligible first when it is analysed into its constituent concepts.' For it is true that the concept is reality and the idea appearance, and I should almost agree that the concept is the only object of knowledge. But I defy Mr Moore to show a case of a concept which is actually known; and if he presents cases of such, I am certain that he has taken the shadow for the substance, the idea for the concept. It is true that existence (for which we substitute here *reality*) is itself a concept and true that we can define reality only by a reference to truth — for this only means that our only criterion for the degree of reality of a given appearance is the criterion of consistency and inclusiveness; it certainly does not mean that because reality is a concept it is known. What collateral can Mr Moore put up on behalf of such 'knowledge'?

We have thus seen in what way an idea is an identical reference and in what way it is related to the concept: the idea may precede the articulate thought, and likewise the concept may be said as an existent to precede thought, although its existence is not known of until late in the development of language. I turn accordingly to consider the relation of idea to image and mental presentation, and to the aspect of idea as a mental sign or symbol. And here I find serious difficulties with Mr Bradley's views, difficulties which may be due to my own obtuseness, but in which I seem to find my objection supported by the objections of Mr Moore and Mr Hoernle. 'For logical purposes ideas are symbols, and they are nothing but symbols (*Logic*, p. 3). . . . A symbol has 1. existence; 2. content. By a sign we understand any sort of fact which is used with a meaning. The meaning may be part of the original content, or it may have been discovered or even added by a further extension. . . . P. 4: A sign is any fact that has a meaning, and meaning consists of a part of the content, original or acquired, cut off, fixed by the mind, and considered apart from the existence of the sign.'[7]

In what sense is an idea a sign? This seems a most treacherous statement. A sign has its existence beside its content, and it is just this separate existence — the fact that the sign might be misinterpreted or simply not recognized as a sign at all, which makes it a sign and not an identity. Take some of the examples of sign which Bradley mentions. A flower may become the sign or symbol of an emotion; the fox is the symbol of cunning. The meaning of these signs consists in a 'part of the content (original let us concede in the case of the fox, acquired in the case of the flower) cut off and considered apart'. Now does an idea refer to reality as fox refers to cunning? The quality to which the fox or the flower refers is something known or knowable otherwise than through the fox or the flower. And this is the case even when the sign is not fox in general, but as, let us say, when a withered flower is the sign of a particular moment in our history. The flower may be the only reminder we have of this moment, but it is in fact because of its essential heterogeneity with the event that it is able to replace itself and us with it, in the past. A flower may be the sign of an idea, but how can an idea be the *sign* of a reality? Such a view would surely lead us to a representational theory of knowledge.

The idea certainly has a sort of existence apart from the reality to which it refers, but the apartness is of a special sort and may easily be misunderstood. There may or may not be a mental content beside the meaning, but Mr Hoernle is certainly right in holding the meaning to be no part of this content (*op. cit.*, p. 74): 'We have nothing to qualify reality with except the contents of our minds, our imagery, which we "divorce" and "cut loose" from its existence in the mind so as to weave a garment for reality out of it.' The meaning is the idea, and the idea may be continuous with or in a sense dependent upon 'mental content', but so far as it is idea, is distinct therefrom. We must ask then (1) in what way idea is not that which it means, and (2) in what way it is not the 'mental' images and conditions.

The contrast between meaning and reality is not so apparent when the reality intended is a present sense perception as in some other cases. In memory, for example, or anticipation, there may be the consciousness of an intended reality and of a present meaning which are not co-existent in time. The reality is there, and the 'mental state' here. And inasmuch as this present state may omit the greater part of what was present to the reality which is remembered, and may likewise add or distort, we are accustomed to form in imagination the notion of a perfect idea of the past experience identical in content with the experience itself, and differing only in that it is present as a memory instead of past as an experience. The effort of memory, in this case, would be to identify itself with the past experience, and the completion of the process would be hallucination. This I suppose is the natural view — based upon comparison of cases of greater and less success in recollection — but it is simply a tissue of contradiction. It assumes, in the first place, that memory is always of images, whereas it is frequently of objectives, which may tend, it is true, to reinstate the imaginal conditions of the experience, but which may be independent of these conditions both for appearance and for certitude. And it may assume in the second place, a reinstatement of objects in a way which implies a point of view which was never actual. What we attend to in perception is one group of objects; what we attend to in memory is a different group: not, as in perception, the object as in itself it really is, but its image. Not that there are two distinct entities, the object and its image — the difference is not one of physical objects, but of intended objects. In perception we intend the object; in recollection we intend a complex which is composed of image and feeling. We do not intend to remember simply the object, but the object as we remember it. And this new object is much more *the experience* than *the past object*, for we try to remember how we felt toward the past object.

On the Distinction of 'Real' and 'Ideal'

It will be said: this feeling-object which we intend is simply a moment in the reinstatement of the total situation, the consummation of which operation would be the presence of the object as object and of the feeling as feeling. To recall feeling we are often told, is merely to live it over; it cannot be known or remembered, but only felt. And to this objection we can retort that hallucination is not the satisfaction and consummation of memory, but its disease. And so far as the feeling is merely felt, so far as the situation is merely lived over again, it is not a case of memory at all. We are attempting to recall, let us say, a public address which we have heard. If memory were simply a restoration of the past, we might expect to recall first the words or fragment of the sentences which the speaker uttered, rather than the sense which we extracted therefrom. For these sounds which he uttered take precedence in time of the meaning; the meaning, to use Meinong's phrase, is a *zeitverteilter Gegenstand*, and the fact that we recall the meaning, in most cases, before we recall the actual words, would imply that the past presents itself in a different time-order than that of the objective time in which the events are held to have taken place. Now in most cases the meaning is what we want; if we had to live through the whole speech again to re-extract the meaning, we should find it very inconvenient. And the meaning can hardly be said to exist in time as the spoken words exist. Furthermore, the meaning intended in attention to the speaker is not the same as the meaning intended in recollection. In hearing we aim at the meaning of the speaker — in memory we aim at the meaning which we drew from his words. And the same distinction holds good, though it is less apparent, even with the speaker's words: for we intend in the one case the words as spoken, in relation to the speaker, and we intend in the other the words as we heard them. And the words in this aspect, were never an actual object of perception; they have their existence only in memory. The past which we aim at is the experience of an ideal individual, who should have been both internal and external to ourselves, who should have both known and experienced the past to which *in a very loose sense* our memory may be said to 'refer'.

On the Distinction of 'Real' and 'Ideal'

In short, it appears that the past in the sense in which it is supposed to be recalled, in popular psychology, simply never existed; the past lived over is not memory, and the past remembered was never lived. But it will again be objected, if there is not a partial identity, and the possibility of degrees of identity, between the idea and an objective past reality, how is the idea to be distinguished from an idea of imagination? And it may be answered that there is an identity — not the sort of identity which we find between two objects, but that which can be found between two aspects. The past as lived and the past as remembered are in fact one and the same in intention, although in fact there is no reason to say either that they are the same or different. In order to make either statement, one would have to show a point of fact to which both refer, or one to which one refers and the other does not; and this identical viewpoint does not occur. You either live the past, and then it is present, or you remember it, and then it is not the same past as you once lived: the difference is not between two objects, but between two points of view. Two points of view may intend the same thing without there being any 'thing' which is the same. The sameness is a function of the two points of view. But there may, as we have seen, be a certain amount of discrepancy without any impeachment of memory, as when we 'remember' as the statement of a speaker what is actually a present inference from what we heard.*

* My remarks on the memory-image are I think thoroughly in accord with the conclusions of Titchener; but for me differences are essential which for Titchener appear to be only accidental (*Text-book of Psychology*, Part II, pp. 418-19). 'Is it not something of a paradox that the memory-image should be thus variable and instable? At first thought, yes: because we are ready to accept, from popular psychology, the notion that an image is a memory-image of itself, in its own right; and if that were the case, the image must of necessity copy or reproduce the perception. On reflection, no: because the image is, after all, made into a memory-image by the feeling of familiarity. So there is no reason in the world why it should copy the original experience. All it has to do — if we may ourselves talk a popular psychology — is to mean that experience (the meaning is given as the context of associated ideas and attitude) and to be recognized as meaning it. Suppose for a moment that memory-images were just weaker copies of the earlier perceptions, and nothing less or more: our mental life would, so far as we can imagine it, be an inextricable confusion of photographically accurate records. It is, in reality, because the image breaks up, because nervous impressions are telescoped, short-circuited, inter-changed, suppressed, that memory, as we have

On the Distinction of 'Real' and 'Ideal'

The identity in question is an ideal identity, a relation which exists only in relation with other (in fact, with all the other) identities in the series: it is an identity supported, if you like the phrase, by the will. You have a past experience and a present memory and, if these were all that existed, even they would not exist for they would constitute two utterly disparate worlds. But you have also an experience *b* and a memory *B*, and so on, and when you have the two alphabets given and only then you have some standard for comparison. The reference of each memory is not given separately, but you are, in a sense, given the whole series first. You cannot say simply 'A is identical with *a*', but you say 'A is identical with *a*, with regard to the identity of *B* with *b*' and vice versa.[8]

The idea, if the foregoing remarks have any cogency, is not a glass through which we descry a past reality, but the idea of a past reality is itself the object, an object which is not past in the sense of a past object of experience, and which is not present in the sense of a present object. It may appear a paradoxical statement, but it is not altogether untrue to say that the object of a memory is the memory itself: meaning only that we must distinguish between the object of the memory and the object of our attention when we remember. In memory, consequently, there is no more divorce between idea and reality than in any other kind of apprehension; the reality is our memory of a past experience, the idea is the reality in so far as we find the idea satisfactory; and when the idea fails to satisfy, we identify it with some other reality of memory or imagination. And the more or less figurative expression 'some other reality' must not mislead us: the operation consists simply in recognizing the idea for what it already is. How much this qualification explains is a question which introduces us to the dangerous problem of error, and this problem I shall

memory, is at all possible. The remark has often been made that, if we did not forget, we could not remember. That is true. But we may go even farther and say that, if the mental image could not decay [cf. Hobbes] it could not either be the conscious vehicle of memory.'

My claim is that it is a bad metaphor to speak of the change from percept to memory-image as a decay. There is an alteration, not only in fullness and order, but in content. There are two essentially different points of view.

have to postpone till I have gathered in several other floating embarrassments. I should like now to offer some remarks on the relation of idea and reality when the reality is an anticipated event and when it is an imaginary event or object.

It is obvious that an image located in the future cannot intend the real event, and the theory which possessed some plausibility in the case of memory cannot here apply. In remembering, we have seen, we have a memory which with respect to other memories refers to a particular reality. In the case of an idea located in the future, there is no such correspondence to be found, for the anticipated event may never realize itself. Ideas of anticipation, accordingly, occupy a place between ideas of memory and ideas of imagination. Such ideas may vary in two ways: in the degree of their realization, and in the degree of their connection with the present. This connection, again, may vary in two ways: the idea may be associated with the present, and spring therefrom, either in virtue of its probability or in virtue of its interest. And here is a line of demarcation between anticipation and imagination: a purely imaginary event can never really be set in the future, for such a disposition of ideas implies a continuity with the real existence of the subject, and a 'future' which has not such continuity is no future at all, but might as well be called past. An author can imagine, if you like, what 'might' happen to his characters in the sequel, but such events are either such as the author can imagine himself making to happen, or such as he imagines the characters themselves as anticipating or such as he accepts or rejects. And if I present to myself the figure of a centaur or dryad as existing 'in the future', I do one of two things. I either throw myself direct into a visionary world, which I proceed to qualify by the term 'future', or I qualify present reality and the idea of centaur so as to make the latter to me a real possibility. And the imaginary here mentioned is not as future imaginary; it is the real future of an imaginary present. An anticipated idea, then, cannot be wholly imaginary, and on the other hand it cannot essentially refer to an event which becomes actual. These observations seem so obvious that I must apologize for offering them.

On the Distinction of 'Real' and 'Ideal'

As to the degree of realization, it is not in principle involved. For we have seen that the degree of 'identity' between the memory and its intended real experience is not a question; and here, from the point of view of the idea, we are concerned only with possibility and interest. Though the difference of principle between ideas of the future and ideas of imagination is clear, yet the difference of fact is often hard to determine. We must of course consider an idea as possible, but we may so consider it with a greater or less degree of evidence, as we are moved by interest (including of course fear) or by knowledge: an idea which may appear to an outsider a pure imagination, possesses fatality for one crazed by fear or passion. It has frequently been said that we never desire what we think absolutely inapprehensible: it is however true that some of our sharpest agonies are those in which the object of desire is regarded as both possible and imaginary, in which in fact the *aspro martiro* is due to the irony of the contrast: the mistress exists as possessed in the real world of anticipation of the disappointed lover, while present reality is forcing itself in upon him with the conviction that this possession is imaginary. Images of future satisfaction to which we looked forward with confidence, we are constantly compelled to consign to the limbo of imagination; and we frequently forget that they were not imaginary in their genesis. The principle of the idea of anticipation, in short, I take to be this. The present as experience is as we have seen (Chapter I) indefinable and in this sense unknown, but its character, and ultimately its existence depend upon the internal qualification of real by ideal; and in this sense the present is ideal construction, and an ideal construction in which ideal constructions of the past and future are integral. These ideas do not qualify a real past and future, for there is no real past or future for them to qualify; past and future are as such themselves ideal constructions. Ideas of the past are true, not by correspondence with a real past, but by their coherence with each other and ultimately with the present moment; an idea of the past is true, we have found, by virtue of relations among ideas. Similarly, an idea of the future is not applied to the real complex which shall

54

represent the realization or falsification of this idea. The present of ideal construction, the present of meaning and not simply of psychical or physical process, is really a span which includes my present ideas of past and future. The reality of the future is a present reality, and it is this present future-reality of which our ideas of anticipation are predicated, and with which they are identified. 'She must weep or she will die' is a statement *not* about the *real future* (which would be a contradiction) but about the *real future*.[9] We are not to say that one of these ideas is realized and the other left floating 'like Mahomet's coffin'[10]; there is really but one idea, and that is predicated of a present future with which it is identical. The reality is immanent to the idea, or else the idea is not the idea of that reality.

If the last statement is true at all, it is true of the ideas of imagination as well as of any other. I shall state very briefly what I take to be the principle here involved, leaving the full discussion of the existence of unreal objects to a later chapter, in connection with the theories of Meinong. If I figure to myself the character of a personage of fiction, it is not true to say that there is no real object to which the idea means to 'correspond'. The distinction between real and unreal is practically useful but metaphysically baseless and indefensible. The character of fiction is imperfectly real because it is imperfectly ideal. And the round square, so far as it is idea (and I do not mean image) is also real. It is not unreal, for there is no reality to which it should correspond and does not. If there were to be such a reality, one would have to have an idea of it — and this idea which you call unreal is the only idea of it which you can present. The detailed discussion of this point I shall take up in connection with the problem of content, object, act, and presentation. The complete idea is the reality, and it is not until the idea realizes itself, and thus becomes really ideal, that we can really trace its ideal connections. When the poet says

I lived with shadows for my company

she is announcing at once the defect and the superiority of the world she lived in. The defect, in that it was vaguer, less of an idea, than the world of others; the superiority, in that the shadows pointed toward a reality, which, if it had been realized, would have been in some respects, higher type of reality than the ordinary world — compared to which the ordinary world would be less real, and which the ordinary world might be said to 'mean'.[11]

The question in what sense an idea is 'meaning', may now be resolved. I accept Bradley's definition of a judgment as the predication of an idea of reality, and I agree that this idea is one whole. And in the article to which I have frequently referred ('Floating Ideas') he has laid down the general doctrine of the relation of real and ideal. But I maintain that for metaphysical purposes at least (*Logic*, p. 3) the notion of idea as symbol is quite inadequate. An idea is not a symbol as a fox is of cunning, or an anchor of hope. You cannot so isolate existence and meaning, in the case of ideas. And to say that an idea is an identical reference is only partially true. There is however a sense in which it may be said that idea is meaning. We may say, in one way, that every idea means itself; its ideality consists in its 'pointing toward' its realization, or (we have found it to be the same thing) toward its own idealization, Hence an idea as contrasted with reality, is something which cannot be grasped — for it can only be described in terms of that reality — in which case you have the reality and not the idea; or it must be described in terms of some other reality — in which case it has lost its meaning, and is no longer the same idea. The existence of idea, then, in contrast with the real, is only in the process, eluding our pains; for as soon as you touch it, you find that the whole world resolves itself into ideas — or into reals. The idea is, as idea, Act; and how far Act can be made an object, together with its relation to content, presentation, and object (*Inhalt, Vorstellung,** Gegenstand*) will form the subject of the ensuing chapter.

---

* Should I apologize for the fact that my use of 'idea' does not correspond with that of any author with whom I am acquainted? I have tried to show in the foregoing that *idea* should not be used indifferently with *concept* or with *image*, and *presentation* has a rather different use from either.

CHAPTER III

The Psychologist's Treatment
of Knowledge

The conclusion derived from the two preceding sections has been that within the whole which is experience and is reality there is a distinction of real and ideal (within which is included the distinction of real and unreal): a distinction which turns out to be appearance and not real, inasmuch as the real is largely ideal, and the ideal is also real; a distinction, however, which in a sense supports reality.* For it is by this distinction that the word reality contains any meaning. We have found that reality is in a sense dependent upon thought, upon a relative point of view, for its existence; for ultimately the world is completely real or completely ideal, and ideality and reality turn out to be the same. And we found that the ideal can never be set over against the real absolutely, but tends to run, either forward or back, into the real which it intends, or the real out of which it may be said to be made: for both these reals are after all nothing but itself at another stage of development. It will be evident that the problem of error, in such a theory, becomes a very clamorous one. To approach this problem we must examine more narrowly the various moments of the process of apprehending an object: and inquire whether the distinction of real and ideal, as we have found its general principle, corresponds to the distinction of object and act, or of object and presentation. The nature of mental 'activity' and the operation of categories must be discussed. And the

---

* Mr Bradley does not commit himself to the assertion that non-relational experience is impossible, but it is implicit in his position. This, of course, is not in conflict with the other assertion that all experience is in the end non-relational.

question, much agitated in recent years* of the subject-matter of psychology, must be agitated again.

The distinction between real and ideal in psychology takes several forms. On the one hand, it may be said, is external reality, and on the other mental content, which is ideal in so far as it intends that reality and has reality of its own as well; and which, under the aspect of that reality of its own, can be studied by the psychologist. Or we may deny the possibility of a valid distinction between content and external reality, and distinguish only between object and act or conation. Or we may deny activity to consciousness altogether, and assemble existents in one complex or another. Or we may say that reality consists of elements of sensation, the rest being ideal construction. Or there is the view of Mr Bradley, for whom everything is in a way psychical, and for whom therefore the distinction between object and act is not identical with that between an internal and an external reality but is reducible to the problem of knowing one's own mind.

The questions involved are these: in an act of apprehension is there a part which is strictly mental and a part which is strictly external? and even if the distinction can be made, can it be made sharply enough to give us a class of objects which can form a separate science, psychology? and the ultimate question is: is there a problem of the possibility of knowledge as well as that of the morphology and structure of knowledge?

There are two terms of psychology, which imply unexamined assumptions, and one of which at least has undergone the fire of recent realism: 'mental content', and 'psychical process'. The first is an assumption still of the majority of psychologists. The presentation of an external object may or may not 'agree' with that object, but in the cases where we assume a complete agreement or identity, the presentation is like a point at which the

---

* I refer to the articles in *Mind* by Bradley, Prichard, Joseph, Stout, and Joachim; to the articles in the *Proc. Arist. Soc.* and in the *British Journal of Psychology* by Alexander; and articles in the *Proc. Arist. Soc.* by Stout, Hicks and Dumville. I shall also refer to writings of Meinong, Messer and Lipps (especially the latter's *Inhalt und Gegenstand*).

circumferences of two circles are in contact: the one point may be taken twice over in two diverging contexts. Thus Miss Wodehouse declares (p. 13) that content has one context, while object has another. The one is continuous with mental history, the other with external or physical. And Witasek states the theory in a more extreme way (which Miss Wodehouse would probably not accept) when he says (p. 3): 'a stone die is hard and cold, grey and heavy and angular: the presentation thereof, the thought or memory of the die, has none of these characteristics, and cannot have them — it merely itself contains, over again, the presentation of hard and cold and so on. . . . My *inner picture* . . . of the tree . . . is known only to myself.'* Hofler is saying the same thing when he makes the distinction: 'Physical phenomena are presented as spatial, and indeed in extended fashion, as located at a place; all mental phenomena are *unspatial*.'** Stout (*Manual*, p. 58) says: 'If I perceive a triangle, my perception is not triangular, — it is not made up of lines and angles.' And the same view is implied by Titchener, when he says (*Text-book*, p. 37): 'The psychologist seeks, first of all, to analyse *mental experience* [italics mine] into its simplest components.'

This assumption that references or meanings can be handled in the same way as the objects to which they refer, an assumption which so far as I can find, it is hardly thought necessary to defend, is an assumption which I believe to have very slight foundation.***

* 'Ein steinerner Würfel ist hart und kalt, grau und schwer und eckig; die Vorstellung von ihm, der Gedanke, die Erinnerung an ihn, hat nichts von diesen Eigenschaften, und kann nichts davon haben — sie enthält nur selber wiederum die Vorstellung von hart und kalt und anderem. . . . [M]ein *inneres Bild* [italics mine] vom Baume . . . das kenne ich allein. . . .'

** 'Physische Erscheinungen werden als räumlich und zwar, 1. als ausgedehnt, 2. als an einem Orte befindlich vorgestellt; alle psychische Erscheinungen sind *unräumlich*.'

*** As I am in this discussion particularly indebted to Mr Prichard I will ask permission to quote at some length from *Kant's Theory of Knowledge*, pp. 125–6: '[T]he tendency to think that the only object or, at least, the only direct object of the mind is something mental still requires explanation. It seems due to a tendency to treat self-consciousness as similar to consciousness of the world. When in reflection we turn our attention away from the world to the activity by which we come to know it, we tend to think of our knowledge of the world as a reality to be

The Psychologist's Treatment of Knowledge

I wish to consider several typical instances of the theory, and point out the untenable postulates upon which it rests. I would then discuss certain ambiguities in the position of Mr Bradley in this matter, and sketch a theory which appears to me more consistent with his metaphysical views. And first I should like to offer a tentative definition of Fact. A fact, I would submit, is a point of attention which has only one aspect, or which can be treated under one aspect. A fact, then, is an ideal construction, and has its existence within a more or less variable sphere of practical or scientific interest. It is not a judgment simply, but an objective asserted ('it is a fact that'); it contains an internal judging and an external recognizing of the validity of the judgment. Thus when I say 'Velasquez painted this portrait of Philip II' there is as yet no fact expressed; when I say 'it is a fact that V., etc.', or 'it is true that — ' or 'I know that — ' I am concerned with fact. There is a sphere of historical Reality which is taken for granted, a sphere existing in such a way that the judgment referred to must be either right or wrong, and this sphere we will call 'matter of fact'. And if this judgment is made upon the ground of internal evidence, there may be as well a sphere of aesthetic values taken for granted. Facts are not merely found in the world and laid together like bricks, but every fact has in a sense its place prepared for it before it arrives, and without the implication of a system in which it belongs the fact is not a fact at all. The ideality essential to fact means a particular point of view, and means the exclusion of other aspects of the same point

apprehended similar to the world which we apprehended prior to reflection. We thereby implicitly treat this knowledge as something which, like the world, merely *is* and is not the knowledge of any thing; in other words, we imply that, so far from being knowledge, i.e. the knowing of a reality, it is precisely that which we distinguish from knowledge, viz. a reality to be known, although — since knowledge must be mental — we imply that it is a reality of the special kind called mental. But if the knowledge upon which we reflect is thus treated as consisting in a mental reality which merely *is*, it is implied that in this knowledge the world is not, at any rate directly, object of the mind, for *ex hypothesi* a reality which merely *is* and is not the knowledge of anything has no object. . . . The root of the mistake lies in the initial supposition — which, it may be noted, *seems to underlie the whole treatment of knowledge by empirical psychology* [italics mine] — that knowledge can be treated as a reality to be apprehended, in the way in which any reality which is not knowledge is a reality to be apprehended.'

60

of attention. There is a sense, then, in which any science — natural or social — is *a priori*: in that it satisfies the needs of a particular point of view, a point of view which may be said to be more original than any of the facts that are referred to that science. The development of a science would thus be rather organic than mechanical; there is a fitness of the various facts for each other, with that instinctive selection and exclusion which is a characteristic of human personality at its highest. Thus the character of a science, like the character of a man, may be said both to be already present at the moment of conception, and on the other hand to develop at every moment into something new and unforeseen. But it will have, from its crudest beginnings, a character to which (though it may belie all our verbal definitions) it will always remain consistent.

Accordingly we may well look, without seeking to formulate narrowly, for the traits of psychology's maturity in the features of infancy. And I have been unable to discover, in the first place, that any scientific individuality is possible as 'reference or meaning', or that you can conjure up one by the magic word 'presentation'. The presentation, I shall argue, is identical with the object from the point of view of the experiencing subject, and from this point of view you have, in metaphysics, no appeal. If we come to find anything more real (as common sense tells us that we must) our criterion will not be an arbitrary division of experience and an arbitrary neglect of the individual, but a theory of degrees of reality. And it is only this arbitrary division which gives us the puzzles of immanent and transcendent object, of unreal and imaginary.

'Whatever constituents of our total experience at any moment', says Stout (*Manual*, p. 57), 'directly determine the nature of the object as it is perceived or thought of at that moment, belong to the cognitive side of our nature, and are called *presentations*.' I do not know in the first place exactly what limits Mr Stout feels justified in setting to the 'total experience at any moment'; for this definition would surely not exclude physiological process or logical category. Does he mean the 'content of consciousness'? But a so-called content of consciousness is not, any more than the world of knowledge, a mere collection of entities in which being and being known is identical; so far as they refer to their objects they are not themselves known, and so far as they are made objects of knowledge they no longer refer to objects.* The sensation of red, as cognitive, is not a presentation, but awareness of a red object, an object which is not in any case mental. What do we mean when we turn our attention from a red object to a sensation red? We are, I think, simply diverting attention from a variously determined object to a uniquely determined one. The so-called real object is in Mr Stout's words 'circumscribed and directed by a plexus of visual and other presentations'.[12] He should either say, I think, that the object *is* this plexus, or admit that even a single sensation circumscribes and directs an object. I cannot see why two or more sensations should give us the object when one does not. For Mr Stout admits that the object may really be presented. 'We may say, if we choose, that the object itself is *presented*, but we must not say that it is a presentation; and when we say that it is presented, it is better to say that it is presented *to* consciousness, than that it is presented *in* consciousness' (*An. Psych.*, I, p. 47). I fail to discern the difference; even if consciousness could have perceptions both outside and inside, I do not know how it would succeed in distinguishing one kind from the other. The difference is simply this: a 'red object' is an object which is otherwise known than by the quality red; it is an object which has been given a determined place in an order. The sensation is an object which has not yet thus been placed. It is incorrect, then, to say that we can have sensations of redness; redness is a concept; or to say that we have sensations of red. The sensation is of a red *something*, a red spot or area. And the discovery that the cause of the sensation is a pathological irritation does not affect the objectivity of the sensation in the least. The red 'that' was there, and the fact that the object cannot be further defined and verified does not make it any the less object.

* As has been ably pointed out by Mr Prichard and I believe by Professor Cook Wilson.

The Psychologist's Treatment of Knowledge

The distinction between object and presentation can be made, as we have seen, in another way: the perception of a triangle, says Stout, is not triangular; the idea of a stone, says Witasek, is not hard and grey. This statement I believe to be in a sense false, and in a sense mere juggling with words. You argue that because idea and object are different, the idea cannot have the physical qualities of the object, and the fact that the idea cannot have these qualities goes to show that there is an 'idea' different from the object. The confusion of course is between reference and existence: the idea is conceived to have an existence apart from its object. This existence, as I have attempted to show in the preceding chapter, is simply the fact of its reference. This fact (which is an objective) cannot be said to be triangular or grey (though it may be hard) — but the fact thus isolated is not the idea; the fact of the reference of the idea must not lead us to speak of the idea as a fact; the idea is only matter of fact. And indeed we may say that the idea is an *abstraction from itself* — for the whole idea is (and yet cannot be) the reality, the idea, and the fact of reference of the idea.

When we say, then that the idea or the perception of a triangle is not triangular, we mean only the fatuity, that the fact of reference is not triangular. And as I have attempted to show in the preceding chapter, the idea (and the perception) is always in a sense identical with the reality which it intends. There can be for a perception, as we have seen, an indeterminate object; there can as well be a mistaken object, and in this way, when the same perception seems to be transferred from one object to another, we are tempted to say that the perception exists and is an object itself apart from any intended object. We have all had the experience of remarking a large bird in the distance, and discovering that it is a small insect a foot or two away. Here we say was a perception which has attached to two different objects. It is not so. There are two different perceptions, the second more consistent with a 'world', but no more closely attached to an object presented *to* consciousness than is the first. There cannot, that is, be a perception of an object if the object perceived is not really

63

there. And when you attempt to consider this 'presentation' apart from any prejudice as to the nature of reality you are committed to a contradiction. You must treat the perception either as an illusion or as true. Apart from one or the other of these two points of view the perception simply does not exist. Any attempt to separate percept from object merely doubles the object. A perception cannot be an object for psychology in the sense in which Mr Stout would have it, because it involves two irresoluble points of view.

I confess that I am confused rather than enlightened by Mr Stout's rejoinder to Mr Prichard (*Mind*, April 1907). He says: 'For Psychology, the *esse* of the facts with which it deals is *percipi* in the sense that it considers things only in so far as they are at any moment known, or in so far as they come to be known ... to an individual mind, and so enter into further relations both to the knowing mind, and to each other.' The fallacy of this statement, if I read it rightly, is as follows. The *esse* of no fact can be *percipi*. Now is psychology really considering 'things only in so far as they are at any moment known ... to an individual mind'? For so far as they are known to an individual mind they *are* simply, and that's an end of it. And if as psychologists, we inquire into the nature of things as known to another individual mind, we are doing much more than we think: we are abstracting from them one kind of reality which they had for this mind, and substituting therefor another kind — namely, their reality as related to this mind. In Mr Stout's well-known instance, the man enjoying a cigar, there are, following out his definition, three cigars present:

1. The cigar known to the smoker.
2. The (cigar known to the smoker) as known to the psychologist.
3. The cigar known to the psychologist, in the role of private citizen.

Now if we content ourselves with being psychologists and not epistemologists, we have no warrant for identifying these three cigars. And Mr Stout not only insists upon the different points of view (the experiences of individual minds) but holds the inconsistent belief that psychology can exhibit the construction of the external world — that it can first abstract wholly from reality, and then piece reality together out of the abstractions.

Again, Mr Stout's beliefs in regard to the nature of sensations are far from clear. In the reply to Mr Prichard he says (*ibid.*, p. 241): 'What we [himself and Dr Ward] refer to when we speak of sensation is something apprehended as distinct from the act of apprehension. . . . Sensations . . . are . . . objects or, as Ward would say, "presentations".' This seems clear enough, though we may be disconcerted in referring back to the preceding page to find that a presentation, as the word is used by Dr Ward, is 'whatever is known *qua* known, whether directly or indirectly'. There is an ambiguity about the phrase 'known *qua* known'. It may mean: 1. from the point of view of the knower; 2. from the point of view of an observer regarding the knower in the act of knowing. Now on turning to Stout's article 'Are Presentations Mental or Physical? A Reply to Professor Alexander', (*Proc. Arist. Soc.*, 1908–9, a year later than the reply to Prichard), we find stated on page 245: 'Sensations . . . cannot be merely objects if they are capable of entering into the constitution of properly subjective states.' And on page 246: 'Can Retentiveness be explained if presentations are Physical?' And referring to the *Manual*, we find that (p. 119) 'It is better to restrict the term *sensation* to the special form of consciousness which accompanies the actual operation of stimulus'. I do not know what a 'special form of consciousness' is; the phrase is at best hardly luminous. And when I find the author in one and the same article (*Mind*, p. 241, April 1907) stating that a sensation is an object, and later suggesting (*ibid.*, p. 242) that an (external) object may be made up of sensations, as a plant is of root, stem, leaves, etc., I conclude that I know neither what is sensation nor what is object.

The confusion results, I think, not so much from there not being several realities to correspond to the several terms, as from the use of terms in a plural marriage to mean several things indifferently: and to the fact that there are not distinct classes of *objects* to correspond to the several (real) distinctions. The former difficulty is peculiar to Mr Stout; the latter is a general difficulty of the subject-matter, and is apparent in a psychologist of a very different school, Professor Alexander. Mr Alexander is equally certain that a field of the psychical may be sharply distinguished from the non-psychical, though he draws the line elsewhere. In several remarkable articles, and notably that 'On Sensations and Images' (*Proc. Arist. Soc.*, 1909–10) he has maintained a conational psychology. (*Proc. Arist. Soc.*, 1908–9): '. . . mind consists of conations, affection being treated as a modality of conation.' And in the article just cited: 'The sentience is mental, but it is held not to vary in quality. The *sensum*, which I shall commonly call sensation, is non-mental.' Similarly (p. 13): 'the imaging is mental, the image physical.' In the attention to a green object, the object of our attention 'may be merely the sensation green' (p. 1).[13]

In contrast to the theory of Mr Stout, such a view has manifest conveniences. It enables us, in the first place, to do away with the equivocal 'presentation' which we have found such a source of embarrassment. Where Stout vacillates between feeling and object, the two are here sharply discriminated. The difficulties of unreal objects, of presentations which present nothing, are apparently avoided. Yet I think that the ultimate objections are much the same after all. In the first place, consider the status of sensation. Mr Alexander appears to assume, like almost everybody else, that we may have a consciousness which is in the strictest sense the consciousness of a sensation, and of nothing else. I have argued (*supra*, p. 62) that a 'sensation of colour' is a loose expression for a perception of a coloured something, and when we think of a colour, it is of a thing not otherwise conditioned than by that colour that we think. Similarly, in the case of a cutaneous pain-sensation, it is of an object conditioned only by that pain-sensation that we think. The sensation, I maintain, is always a way of being conscious of an object, and as we become conscious of this consciousness, it may result in an added determination either of the object or of the self. Hence, on my view, a consciousness of red is on the one hand a red consciousness and on the other hand the consciousness of a red object.

Otherwise, I think, Mr Alexander will find the same difficulty in constructing an object out of sensations as does Mr Stout. A sensation is certainly an object in the sense that it is the object to which it refers; but when we are aware of an object, the sensations through which we come into contact with it do not persist alongside it as independent objects, as on the ultra-objective theory I should expect them to. We seem to find a fallacy which can be attacked thus: *The object of attention and the qualities or conditions of this object cannot be equally objective from the point of view for which they exist as such.*

In a sensation, that is, there are two verbal moments, the -ing and the -ed, which can be discriminated when together but cannot be treated apart. The evidence that they can be discriminated for certain practical purposes is simply this, that when we speak of a sensation, in our quotidian vocabulary we can with perfect propriety have *emphasis* on either the active or the objective aspect, never meaning wholly one or the other in isolation. Sensation-in-itself is in the language of Bradley 'feeling' or experience as more original than consciousness; but sensation in itself is not as such capable of being an object of attention (Chapter I). Sensation and perception, on the theory I have just outlined, are different in concept but in existence different only in degree. Sensation as known is always some degree of crude perception:[14] the moment we speak of 'having a sensation' we have stepped into the theory of knowledge, have posited a self and consequently an external world; it is still sensation, however, in that it is rather a feeling of a peculiar relation than a characterization of either subject or object.

The situation of the separate sensations, then, with regard to the developed object, is this: the sensations cannot be objects on the same plane as the developed object, since it is to this object, and not as before, to themselves (as by the vagueness of their reference they may loosely be said to do) that they refer. They are the ways of being conscious — the *content* — of this object, and in a sense the total experience may be said to be, on a higher plane, a fuller sensation of a remoter object (and so on). In other words, there is a constant transcendence of object into reference, and the absolutely objective is nowhere found. This, I think, furnishes a pertinent criticism of Mr Alexander. In a world so objective as that of Mr Alexander one cannot have a genuine object presented to one. ('On Sensation and Images', p. 15): 'Fully realise that perceiving a thing means that mind and the thing are together in the same sense as the table and the floor are together, and you understand that the imagination of the table means that the mind and the table are together; but the table in its imagined form, with imperfections and added elements.' I do not see how they can be together unless it is admitted that the object is only the compound of sensations — a position which may lead to Berkeley, and certainly leads to nominalism; (*Con. Psych.*, p. 253)[15]: '. . . a thing as perceived contains besides sensory elements other elements present to the mind only in ideal form. . . . But the ideal elements are themselves objective and non-mental. They exhibit their true relation to the sensory elements in the course of the perceptual process itself.' I do not think that we ought to say that a thing is made up of sensory elements and ideas, as a pastry is made up of the right ingredients and good cooking. I do not think that it is true that we can or do attend to both sorts of elements at the same time in the same way. It is true, if you like, that the ideal elements are non-mental, but their relation with the real elements is one of mutual reference and implication; and in a world composed solely of objects I can find no room for implication. The picture which certain masses of colour 'imply' is just as 'objective' as the colour-sensations, but not objective in the same way; the cognition of the picture means a transition to a different plane of reality. The colour-masses have thus transcended themselves, and ceased to be simply objects.

This introduces us to Mr Alexander's theory of the subject-matter of psychology. Over against sensation the properly mental element is conation. (*Con. Psych.*, p. 243): 'the subject, as given in enjoyment and therefore in the only form in which it enters into psychology is nothing but the continuous tissue of its acts of conation or attention.' Psychology 'will descrive how differently it *feels* or *is enjoyed* when we sense or perceive or will or the like.' Now my difficulty as I have already said, is in understanding what is left when you abstract from a mental state its reference; or what comes to the same thing, what reference is left when you have only the reference. 'In watching a ball which one is trying to catch, the perceptive conation whose object is the approaching ball is that complex of visual and anticipatory tactual conations which issue in movements of the eyes and more particularly of the hands' (*Con. Psych.*, p. 248). I cannot find anything here, once the non-mental or objective elements are abstracted, upon which I can lay my finger. I can see material for psycho-physics, but Mr Alexander insists that psycho-physics is a different field (*ibid.*, p. 248 ff.). I can only understand conation, so far as we may be said to be conscious of it at the moment, and Mr Alexander's conation goes far beyond this point, inasmuch as it is everywhere present — the subject in psychology is a 'continuous tissue' of its acts of conation.

There is no reason for regarding conation as ultimate even from a psychological point of view, unless we are ready to accept a psychology of faculty. And I can see no reason for making will more original than thought. (*Ibid.*, p. 263): '. . . [T]he act of judgment is maintained to be literally an act of will.' The proposition which is the *cognitum* of the judgment is the object willed. It is as possible to state will in intellectual terms, and to say (what I do not believe to be any truer) that will is the self-realization of an idea. The conation, I am ready to admit, exists, but only in a certain context: only with on one side a self to which the conation is attached (but which is never identified with that conation) and on the other side with a real world (real from the point of view of this self, which is all the reality required) which the conation intends. For in willing (and in desiring (Messer) which is another form of conation) some reality is already posited; and in desire the object desired is recognized as somehow real (Bradley). Thus it cannot be wholly true that (*ibid.*, p. 265) '. . . it is in willing that objects ... become known *as* real. ....' And in this relation the conation ceases to be merely a conation.

I cannot help thinking that Mr Alexander's conation tends to find its full reality in physiological process, much as its author may himself deprecate this conclusion. 'There is', he says (*ibid.*, p. 252), 'good reason for believing that these differences [in conation] are really of a spatial character, really are differences *of the locality and direction of the physiological processes* [italics mine] and that that locality and direction are actually enjoyed.' If what we 'enjoy' is the physiological process, then either this process is the object of the enjoyment — which is impossible, as the enjoyment refers to an entity of which we are conscious; or the process *is* the enjoyment — in which case nothing remains surely but to study the process itself. And the tendency toward physiology becomes still more natural if we mean to treat affections (*Proc. Arist. Soc.*, 1908–9, p. 6) 'as a modality of conation'. The necessity for so considering them appears only when we have made conation so substantial as to isolate it from the intended reality, and the con sequence is to make the tertiary qualities aesthetic, and entirely subjective. Now I am prepared to argue that affections are just as objective *if* objectivity is to be absolute and not in any sense a matter of degree — as are sensations. Why should anger be any less objective than pain-sensation? Can we not contemplate our affections as well as our sensations? And if it be said that affections are essentially *wahrnehmungsfluchtig* (perceptually elusive), in contrast to sensation I reply that it appears to me everywhere a matter of degree. And finally I seem to discover that Mr Alexander, like Mr Stout, instead of recognizing everywhere differences of degree, has erected sharp bounds and everywhere transgressed them. One of the bounds is this: 'we contemplate objects, we enjoy our states.'[16] We are then told that 'the fundamental fact of experience informs us that mind is but one thing together with external things ...' and on the next page that panpsychism over looks 'the fundamental difference of mind and things which is expressed by saying that the one is enjoyed and the others con templated' ('The method of metaphysics', pp. 4 and 5).

The Psychologist's Treatment of Knowledge

An equally interesting and more satisfactory demarcation of the field of psychology is that of Lipps (*Inhalt und Gegenstand*). In this essay, in which I find very little to question, Lipps makes the claim that things, and not merely sensations, are given to us. (P. 512): 'A person who sees things . . . is not seeing sensations, or presentations, or perceptions, or experiences. . . .' (P. 513): '. . . sensation . . . is a determination of myself. . . . At the same time the sensing is . . . also, in a manner, a determination of (for example) the blue or red.' There is a relative distinction into 1. Myself; 2. My sensing; 3. That which is sensed, or the content of sensation. What we are conscious of is *object* (p. 520: 'To think something, or think of something, is to have something as an object');* an object which is conditioned by our knowledge of it, because it is *our* object; but which is real, and not mere *Erscheinung* (appearance) — which is, *qua* our object, independent of us. The sensation is at once a *Bestimmung* (determination) of the object and of the *Ich* (the self), a relation between the two which conditions whichever you direct your attention toward.

The *Ich* and its objects then form metaphysically one whole, a whole from which we can abstract in either direction. Qualities in relation to external points of attention give us the realities of practice and natural science; in relation to (*in Beziehung auf*) the *Ich* they give the subject-matter of psychology. Mental states, Lipps insists, have no independent existence: there are simply relations which in our reference constitute the external or objective and in another reference constitute the psychical. *Eigenschaften* (characteristics) in themselves are not objects, not capable of being made a point of attention; they can only be experienced with respect to a point of attention. While normative science — logic, ethics, aesthetics — is 'lyrisch', psychology is 'episch' — gives not *Ausdruck* (expression), but *Bericht* (report). Normative

* (p. 512) 'Wer Dinge sieht . . . sieht nicht Empfindungen oder Vorstellungen oder Perzeptionen oder experiences. . . .' (p. 513): '. . . die Empfindung . . . eine Bestimmung meiner ist . . . Zugleich ist das Empfinden . . . in gewissem Sinne auch eine Bestimmung des Blau oder Rot. . . .' There is a relative distinction into: 1. Ich; 2. mein Empfinden; 3. das Empfundene oder der Empfindungsinhalt. What we are conscious of is *object* (p. 520: Etwas denken, an etwas denken, dies heisst etwas zum Gegenstande haben).

The Psychologist's Treatment of Knowledge

science is the expression of the *ueberindividuelles Ich*, which is in a sense the realization of the limited *Ich*. (P. 663): (The 'supra-individual self') 'is in us, but we are not identical with it. Indeed, so far as we are not, we *ought* to be so. This ought is the call, which is an expression both of the *presence* of this self in us, and of our own *limitations*'. As for empirical psychology, (p. 654) 'it does not, indeed, replace the processes in consciousness, which experience declares to "belong" to the soul, by other conscious processes. But to the occurrence of such processes it adds a variety of determinations, which are of another nature, and so cannot figure in immediate experience: such as stimuli, associations, memory-traces, capacities, character-traits and dispositions. It thereby creates, upon causal principles, a world of the mentally or psychically real, which absolutely transcends, and is thus wholly beyond comparison with, what is given in the immediate experience of the self.'*

This theory has a certain resemblance to that of Ward for whom the subject-matter of psychology does not consist in any particular group of entities, but in the 'whole choir of heaven and earth' from a certain point of view. But there are aspects of Lipps' theory which leads us toward the conclusion that this point of view does not exist. Can *Empfinden* (sensing) be turned inside out and applied to the *Ich* in the same way as to the thing? I am inclined to think that there is a confusion here. I cannot see why, on the ground of the threefold division *Ich — Empfinden — Empfundene* (self — sensing — sensed) and the characterization, which seems to me admirable, of *Empfinden* as a *Bestimmung* (determina-

---

* (The 'ueberindividuelles ich') 'ist in uns, aber wir sind es doch nicht. Eben, soweit wir es nicht sind, sollen wir es sein. Dies Sollen ist die Forderung; und diese ist der Ausdruck zugleich für das Dasein jenes Ich in uns, und für unsere Schranke.' As for empirical psychology (p. 654): 'Sie ersetzt freilich nicht die Bewusstseinserlebnisse, die nach Aussage jener Erfahrung an der Seele "haften", durch andere Bewusstseinserlebnisse. Aber sie fügt zu dem Haben Bewusstseinserlebnissen allerlei Bestimmungen, die nichts dergleichen sind, und darum in der unmittelbaren Erfahrung nicht vorkommen können. So die Reize, die Assoziationen, die Gedächtnisspueren, die Anlagen, Charaktereigenschaften, Dispositionen. Sie baut so dem Kausalgesetze gemäss eine Welt des seelischen oder des psychischen Realen auf, die dem in der unmittelbaren Icherfahrung Gegebenen absolut transzendent, ja damit völlig unvergleichlich ist.'

tion) of both *Ich* and object, any further determination of the status of sensation should be necessary. This one situation is that which it always occupies. I am not, in experience of a colour, treating the sensation as a qualification of the blue or red any more than of myself. However I express myself, I mean only that the sensation is there as a relation between myself and the object, a relation which is internal and goes to make up both self and object. And if you propose to detach this sensation any further from the object and make it a determination solely of the self, then you put it in an entirely false situation. Lipps has already said that the object is really given to us, and the *Ich* really given to us, and that the sensations are not separate objects which stand between us and the object. Now the aim of natural science, I suppose, is simply to dispose of the various appearances which are found to be determinations of the *Ich* and of the real object so far as they are found to have the relation to the subject which they were supposed to have only to the thing — or rather, so far as they are found to have relations and to be distinguishable in thought from the thing. The goal of science, consequently, would be a system of terms in relation, of terms the nature of each of which would be constituted by its place in the system; which would be completely definable by their position, and which would have no characteristics which could be isolated from the system. Every empirical discipline, of course, uses terms the explanation of which would fall outside of that system in which they are explanatory; terms which we require a fresh point of view to analyse.

The attitude of science, then, involves the constitution of a larger and larger limbo of appearance — a larger field of reality which is referred to the subjective side of experience. Economics is appearance for the biologist, biology for the chemist. Similarly, social psychology is appearance to the individual psychologist. It is when we ask what the simple terms of individual psychology are that I am at a loss.

For the relation of appearances (the appearances which condition both self and object) to an ultimate external reality is not the province of any one science to decide, inasmuch as fields of discourse are objective or subjective in different contexts, and as things are non-mental in various ways, so they can be mental in various ways, and if the subject-matter of psychology is to be appearance in relation to the self, we have not one science, but a whole universe of sciences, corresponding to the self as found expressed in the structure of social civilization, in its works of science, in the laws of thought, in image or in sensation.

I think, then, that Lipps has been deceived into conclusions which are inconsistent with his own admirable division of mental and physical, by the tacit assumption that in the sciences other than psychology we abstract from the psychical aspect. The psychical aspect, he has shown himself, is always present: wherever there is the *Ich,* there is a continuity between the *Ich* and its object; not only in the case of perception, but in every case of knowledge. In science we have only abstracted from *one or several spheres of mental reality* — and from physical reality at the same time. We have then done in every science what Lipps asks us to do specially in the case of psychology — considered a field of reality as a condition and expression of the self.

What, if this be true, has Lipps in mind as the field of psychology? Simply, I think, the old chimera, 'states of consciousness', meanings torn from their reference. You have first a mind essentially related to a world. In order to study the mind, you abstract it from the world — but abstract the world with it, and double the world to get a *real* world. You then assert that the first world simply exists as presentation, and that reference is to *your* world, and not to the subject's. And all this comes from the fallacy of treating a difference of aspects as a difference of things.

We meet, however with definitions which make no distinction between mental and non-mental. Thus Miss Wodehouse's (p. 13) content is as objective as object; psychology does not expand the contents of the object but limits them 'because it is interested in their shape' (p. 20). This is an important, and radically different, definition, of the subject-matter of psychology; the external world and the mental world are of exactly the same stuff, and are *ultimately identical, but as experienced are both fragments.*

The Psychologist's Treatment of Knowledge

The world examined by the psychologist is the world which is the content of consciousness in relation to the various elements in the constitution of the subject which condition it; and these elements, I should suppose, may be either that part of the external world which has previously been content of that consciousness, or the physiological and psycho-physical conditions. On the one hand the content is continuous with the whole external universe (p. 21) and on the other hand with the history of that subject. In the latter relation it is the subject-matter of psychology: psychology, accordingly, deals rather with the personal than with the 'psychical'.

This division would seem to give us two clear groups of objects. But I am not convinced that the connections of content may not be reduced to connections of the real world on the one hand and to physiological connections on the other. Memory content must be considered as connected according to the reality remembered and *in the same way as the reality remembered*: that is, the laws which hold of the reality hold of the memory connections in their reference; the laws of the physical world hold of ideas of that world so far as those ideas are real ideas. And so far as those ideas are not real, as from being a specification they are merely a tendency, and from a tendency merely an undifferentiated feeling, the idea is dissolved into physiological conditions. So far as the idea is real, we have seen above, it is not idea; and so far as it is not real it is not idea. This is equally true of ideas of imagination or of ideas of memory. It is not true that the ideas of a great poet are in any sense arbitrary: certainly in the sense in which imagination is capricious, the ideas of a lunatic or an imbecile are more 'imaginative' than those of a poet. In really great imaginative work the connections are felt to be bound by as logical necessity as any connections to be found anywhere; the apparent irrelevance is due to the fact that terms are used with more or other than their normal meaning, and to those who do not thoroughly penetrate their significance the relation between the aesthetic expansion and the objects expressed is not visible.

But it is no wise true that the connections of content are

subjective and peculiarly subject-matter for psychology. They are personal if you like, but a work of imagination is never simply personal. So far as we consider it as *only* personal — i.e. significant only to the author — we explain it not as imagination but as the product of pathological conditions. Thus we are tempted to explain a poem of Mallarmé as we explain dreams, as due to morbid physiological activity. And if it is said that this radical separation would do away with all criticism, we may point out that criticism — involving the circumstances under which a work was produced — is other than psychology in that it includes at every point a reference to a real world with which the other is compared: a procedure which in psychology is inadmissible.

It is sufficient for the purpose of this chapter to have argued that a 'psychological event' can not be torn from its context and be set in a context of other purely psychological events: the problem of the relation of an idea to the real world from the point of view of epistemology must be taken up later. The theory of the idea which I have proposed, and which I believe to be substantially in harmony with Mr Bradley's metaphysics, implies to this point only that the idea, as you try to grasp it as an object, either identifies itself with the reality or melts back in the other direction into a different reality, the reality of its physiological basis. Ideas in relation with the nervous system on the one hand, and with the intended reality on the other, may have a certain existence in epistemology, but have no pretension to a purely 'psychological' existence. And here I find myself in conflict with much that Mr Bradley has had to say on the subject of psychology, especially in his articles on Active Attention, on the Definition of Will, and on a Defence of Phenomenalism in Psychology.[17] The first two articles are explanatory — they substitute for data of immediacy universal connections; we may therefore inquire what these data are. The last article defends a view very similar to those which I have been attacking.

'Psychology', says Bradley (p. 28),[18] 'is to be concerned with psychical events, and such an event is whatever is immediately experienced, either as a whole or as an integral aspect of a whole, and is not for the purpose in hand taken otherwise than as an adjective happening to and qualifying a particular soul. These facts are events because they happen in time, each with a place in the order of the "real world" in general. . . . [T]he meaning of one soul or subject, . . . must be fixed arbitrarily.' (P. 35)[19]: 'You can only explain events . . . by the laws of their happening, and it does not matter for your purpose, so long as these laws work, whether they possess ultimate truth or are more or less fictitious and false.' The difficulty which I find with such a definition lies in the definition of event. Psychical event, it is said, is immediately experienced (distinct from experience). And the question I raise is whether in our conscious life anything is immediately experienced except experience itself. And in the second place the event taken as happening to that particular soul is not the same event from the point of view of that soul, for from the latter point of view the event does not 'qualify' the soul, but qualifies external reality. And if from another point of view, then what is the event? Till you have 'the laws of their happening' how can you be said to have the event? An event, I should suppose, is a *what* — a *that* somehow interpreted, for you must single out some one aspect, you must occupy some point of view not internal to the event, before there is anything of which there can be a law.

Mr Bradley's position involves a parallelism between knowledge as the reality which it intends and knowledge as event in the soul (p. 30).[20] 'To say that ideas and judgements do not happen at a certain time, and that in this sense they fail to be occurrences, seems clearly contrary to fact. . . .'[21] '[T]he idea or the judgement, . . . is assuredly a psychical event. . . . A truth, we may say, is no truth at all unless it happens in a soul and is thus an event which appears in time.'[22] This seems to me to involve a confusion of the psychological point of view with the metaphysical. From the latter standpoint this statement is correct; from the former it seems palpably false. A truth as truth must of course *appear* independent of the soul as experienced in the perception of that truth, and its oneness with the soul (as truth) is a matter of metaphysical unity and not relative to its happening 'in' a soul. A truth as such is quite independent of finite soul, and we may say that it is the finitude of truth which constitntes the finite soul. So far then, as it is an event it is not a truth or a judgment at all. And so far as we are conscious of it as an event it is not in the same sense the 'truth' that we are conscious of. In knowledge then the event of knowledge is not something that enters into consciousness.

It is certainly not from the point of view of the subject that the idea or judgment is an event, and from the subject's viewpoint the only laws of happening are the laws of the world of which he is conscious, while from the outsider's point of view, the only laws are laws which lie beyond the consciousness of the subject. But, it will be said, the subject is conscious of previous ideas and judgments as events in his own career: if he were conscious of them merely as realities apprehended, he would not be aware of his past at all, for it would not be *his* past, but the past of the world. We are constantly passing, that is to say, from the judgment as reality to the judgment as a qualification of ourself — a view which my own account of memory is obliged to support. I again offer, however, the theory of identity there presented, and emphasize the fact that memory is an elaborate and artificial product, which can be treated from the point of view of psychophysics as subject to laws — though only so far as it is not memory — which serves a practical need, and does not pretend to give anything which was ever as such actual. As in memory of an external reality we may have an image which refers to a reality, so in recollection of our own judgment we assert an objective (*that* we judged so and so), an assertion which refers to the judgment as an event but which constitutes it as an event in the act of assertion. For a reference, as I have suggested in several passages, does not everywhere imply the existence of that to which it refers, outside of the reference itself.

Let us say, then that in memory and in the observation of the actions of others we have reference to events which are never as such actual. Have we not here a consistent enough point of view to determine a subject-matter? I would offer two objections. In the first place, these events as psychic phenomena have no laws.

For internally, their relations among themselves are determined only by the real world from the point of view of the subject, and externally by the real world from the point of view of the subject, and externally by the real world from somebody else's point of view[23]; while their mid-way reality is at once greater and less than such as science can grasp. And in the second place the soul is not something definite to which phenomena can be attached all on the same plane, but varies with the meaning which each phenomenon has for it. In order to know what a particular event is, you must know the soul to which it occurs, and the soul exists only in the events which occur to it; so that the soul is, in fact, the whole world of its experience at any moment, while both soul and event transcend that moment. The soul is its whole past so far as that past enters into the present, and it is the past as implied in the present. (*Appearance*, p. 275): 'But at any one time . . . the soul is the present *datum* of psychical fact, plus its actual past and its conditional future.' But I cannot feel satisfied with the statement (*Mind*, 33, p. 29)[24] that 'The soul . . . *is* the dispositions which it has acquired'. 'In saying that the soul has a disposition of a certain kind, we take the present and past psychical facts as the subject, and we predicate of this subject other psychical facts, which we think it may become.' (*Appearance*, p. 276). Now I question whether it is ever a 'psychical' fact which we take as the subject in a disposition. Men are avaricious, generous, vicious, or self-sacrificing, and these qualities I suppose are dispositions. But avarice and generosity are not psychical events but social interpretations of behaviour, behaviour involving the whole organism. What is in the mind of the avaricious or generous man is not avarice or generosity, but a real world qualified in a certain way, and these qualifications are interpreted or introspected as subjective, conditioned by a disposition. But to be 'subjective' is not to be mental, and to be a disposition is ultimately to be a disposition of the whole organism — so that I can see no difference between psychical and physical disposition. For disposition must rest upon something which is actual and this must be a physical structure.

The Psychologist's Treatment of Knowledge

What then as to the doctrine of Mr Bradley (*op. cit.*, *Mind*, p. 41),[25] that an emotion can be attended to? I believe this doctrine to be correct. For on the theory which I have outlined above, pleasure as pure feeling is an abstraction, and in reality is always partially objective: the emotion is really part of the object, and is ultimately just as objective. Hence when the object, or complex of objects, is recalled, the pleasure is recalled in the same way, and is naturally recalled on the object side rather than on the subject side: though it tends (*op. cit.*, *Mind*, p. 44)[26] to instate itself as an active pleasure.*

As to the theory of attention** and the theory of will** I think that they illustrate in detail the objections that I have raised in general. Will, we are told, is the self-realization of an idea; and this explanation I protest against as metaphysics and not psychology. I cannot feel, with regard to an explanation of a faculty which explains it by reference to something which falls outside of consciousness, that such is a psychological explanation. Mr Bradley is concerned with will only in operation: 'With will taken in its full sense I agree that psychology cannot concern itself'(i.e., will as 'standing tendency').[27] And with will as I am aware of will I cannot concede that this definition has anything to do. '[B]ecause I am aware of the idea as itself making the change . . . I am aware also that this change is the work of myself.'[28] But the idea has to be my idea. 'Provided . . . that the idea has remained qualified in my mind as the act of another, it cannot in its proper character, and as such, realize itself in my person.'[29] The fact that the idea has to be my idea seems to give away the whole case; for so far as it is *my* idea it is already willed.

So far as will is not felt, I cannot see any reason for using the concept at all; and so far as it is felt, it requires no explanation and can find none. Mr Bradley's account might be a true account of what goes on when we think that there is will; but in order to be a true account it would have to justify its point of view. Ideas,

* Cf. T. P. Nunn, *Proc. Arist. Soc.*, 1909–10, p. 192.
** 'Active Attention', *Mind*, 1902, No. 41. 'Definition of Will', *Mind*, Nos. 44, 46, 49.

as I have claimed, are not objects, but occupy a half-way stage between existence and meaning. From a purely external point of view there is no will; and to find will in any phenomenon requires a certain empathy; we observe a man's actions and place ourselves partly but not wholly in his position; or we act, and place ourselves partly in the position of an outsider. And this doubleness of aspect is in fact the justification for the use of the term. Another person, and in its degree another *thing*, is not for us simply an object; there is always, I believe, a felt continuity between the object and oneself. The only error lies in regarding this community as due to the common possession of a character which belongs to both subject and object as such, and belongs to each independently. This character is then treated as a thing. But will is not a character of consciousness purely, and it is not at all a character of things as such; it arises only in a conflict, and is in the primitive mind cognized as a character of object as naturally as of subject; so that it is only by a certain degree of abstraction that we come to think of ourselves as willing and of objects as moved by 'forces' — an expression which simply indicates the degree of objectification which we have succeeded in establishing. For these reasons I am inclined to regard will as indefinable and as offering no problem. If we are to have a psychology we must postulate a faculty of will, though we hold will to be finally mere appearance. And such psychology, I think, will be not a scientific but a philosophical discipline. For science deals with objects or with the relations of objects; and will, we have said, belongs to a place half-way between object and subject.

Attention likewise belongs in the class of half-objects. 'Popular psychology', says Titchener (*Psychology of Feeling and Attention*, p. 181), 'regards attention, indifferently, as faculty and as manifestation of faculty.' Here, I suggest, popular psychology is right, for popular psychology (in this sense) is the only psychology that there is. And I believe that Bradley's theory of attention, like Titchener's, is merely an attempt to reduce attention to something else without knowing what that something is. What can we have, in an account of attention, but a description of physiological conditions and a description of the realities apprehended? And there is only attention, I submit, when the conditions and the reality apprehended are confused. That this interfusion is everywhere found does not alter the case. For it is only as felt that the two are confused, and when we turn this feeling into an object the two elements fall apart: 'We cannot attend to several disconnected objects at once; we organize them into a single object' ('Active Attention', p.21).[30] This I believe to be true, but what does it mean? That the world, so far as it is a world at all, tends to organize itself into an articulate whole. The real is the organized. And this statement is metaphysics, so if it comes to us as a novelty it is not psychology. From a psychological point of view, things perceived are connected so far as they are perceived to be connected. If we contemplate several objects, and recognize them as disconnected, they *are* disconnected except for metaphysics, and that is the complete statement of the case. 'But is there then', says Mr Joseph (*Mind*, 1911), 'no such thing as psychology . . . [I]f I were asked what it really is, I should say, not a science, but a collection of more or less detached inquiries, of the result of which philosophy must take account. There are for example inquiries into "double personality" and kindred puzzles, which must affect any theory of the real nature of the individual soul or self; there are experiments about association-time, reaction-time, etc., which help to explain why one man's mind works quicker than another's, but no more throw light on the nature of thinking than the determination of the duration of the crotchet explains the beauty of music. [T]here are more definitely psycho-physical investigations, *e.g.*, into brain-localisation which may have therapeutic value, and of course any facts about the relation of what is mental to what is cerebral are important to a theory of the soul, as of a knower belonging somehow to the same whole with the known.'

I can subscribe to most of this statement. There is certainly an important field for psycho-physics and the study of behaviour, and there are even certain processes where introspection is not without value. But this knowledge, I insist, is knowledge either of physiology, biology, or of the external world, and implies both a real known external world and a real nervous system: for we are not to say that there is a mental content which is mental. There is, in this sense, nothing mental, and there is certainly no such thing as consciousness if consciousness is to be an object or something independent of the objects which it has. There are simply 'points of view', objects, and half-objects. Science deals only with objects; psychology, in the sense of rational or faculty psychology, may deal with half-objects, and metaphysics alone with the subject, or point of view.

CHAPTER IV

The Epistemologist's Theory
of Knowledge

'And there can be really no such science as the
theory of cognition.' (*Appearance*, p. 65)

It has been the conclusion of the foregoing chapter that no
distinct province of mental objects exists as the field of
psychology; that no definition can anywhere be found to
throw the mental on one side and the physical on the other; that
we can never construct the external world from the mental, for the
external is already implied in the mental. The difference between
mental and real, or in the excellent terms of Mr Alexander between the personal and the objective, is one of practical convenience and varies at every moment; so that the terms content
and presentation do not stand for objects of a science but for
aspects of an object. We go on to ask, naturally, whether the
terms with which the epistemologist deals are any more substantial. The distinctions of *immanent* and *transcendent* object,
the terms *real* and *unreal* object, *a priori* and *a posteriori*
knowledge, *phenomenon* and *reality*; *passive apprehension* and
the *activity of consciousness*; these are all terms which have a
certain significance in practical knowledge. But whether thought
has more than a practical validity, whether there is any reality for
thought to reach and whether thought reaches it — the absolute
validity of knowledge — is the problem of the theory of knowledge.
There are evidently three divisions of the question: the problem
of the genesis of knowledge, of the structure of knowledge, and of
the possibility of knowledge. It is, I believe, the position of all
sound idealism, and I believe is the position of Mr Bradley, that
the only real problem is the second. For it may be said, in criticism

of the first problem, that it does not deal with objects of *know-ledge*, and in criticism of the third, that there are no *objects* of knowledge, when the object is treated as a hard and fast reality.

The present chapter is to consider the claims of the third problem, and I will only touch very briefly on the question of the 'growth of knowledge'. While the problem is by no means a negligible one, it can never occupy a place of priority in the theory of knowledge, and the reason is simply this. We are all agreed that the knowledge of the world possessed by man is superior to that possessed by the ape, and that the knowledge of the European is superior to that of the savage, but there remains in this knowledge a *somehow* which is not resolved unless by a theory which is not the outcome of any 'genetic' research. There is recognized in the history which we consider a growth, but it is a growth of 'knowledge' only in the vague or practical sense of the world. In evolution or in the development of the child there is a systematic alteration of values, with an outer expansion and an inner elaboration of content, which we find to be continuous with the values and the content of our own experience. But this alteration is a growth of knowledge only if knowledge is already assumed; and if we make no assumptions about the validity of our own knowledge the growth which we trace is not the growth of knowledge at all, but is the history only of adaptation, if you like, to environment. And in such an account, of course, our knowledge of the environment to which we see the organism adapting itself is taken not as absolute but as relative: we assume only a system of relations such that our knowledge will not be falsified on the plane on which it is knowledge. Nothing, then, is so far known as to the nature of knowledge.

The basis of structural psychology, as we have seen, resolves itself into physiology; and while physiology is by no means irrelevant to the problem of knowledge, its contribution is always indirect. Knowledge being given, physiology can suggest the limitations and give some of the conditions of truth and error; it gives us the background against which knowledge is set and into which it tends to fade. And we are obliged to believe that in a final account the knowledge which we think to possess and the conditions of it will be necessary to explain and complete each other. Meanwhile physiology gives an account, not of our knowledge as knowledge, but under some other aspect. And so long as we have no ultimate and complete knowledge the study of these aspects will remain relevant to epistemology. The intended object is ultimate reality. But in knowing as we experience it the aspect which is knowing is continuous with the other aspects and can never be definitely separated from them at any point. So far as it is knowing, there is no problem and, if there be a problem — of which I am very doubtful — it is constituted by the relation of knowing to the other aspects. Epistemology, therefore, is simply the process by which what is at first knowledge is absorbed into another aspect: knowing becomes known, an activity becomes an object, and the process can be repeated *ad infinitum*.

It is claimed, however, that epistemology occupies a position of unique authority and constitutes a distinct science apart from psychology, physiology, logic, or biology. Epistemology makes the claim of both scientific certainty and metaphysical ultimacy. And it is, I believe, to be repudiated by both scientist and metaphysician; by the first because the external criteria of his science do not concern him, and by the second because he is engaged in the construction of a system, and must place himself at an external point of view from which the wholly internal aspect of knowledge disappears. In a metaphysic such as Mr Bradley's, certainly, there can be no place for a theory of knowledge, for the terms which such a discipline must use have not the requisite substantiality. The problem, it may be remarked, has two parts which are not infrequently confused: the problem of the knowledge of the objects or truths which we do know, and the problem of knowledge in general. In the first we assume the existence of knowledge and inquire into its conditions; in the second we assume nothing and inquire into the possibility of knowledge. And the fact that the two are perhaps never treated wholly independently must not lead us to think that they are not two independent problems. In epistemology we attempt to describe a relation between the knower and the known, to give a description which shall leave both as we find them — which shall, that is, describe an experience which shall still be recognizable after the description; but we ask also the very different question of the validity and meaning of the noetic experience, and this question can only be answered in terms which leave the original experience unrecognizable.

The philosopher who attempts to answer either of these questions must, I believe, be either a dualistic realist or a 'criticist' (which is ultimately the same thing) for I do not propose to classify Kant as anything but a dualistic realist. He assumes that there is a real world, a world of realities of one sort or at most two; he then inquires how we come to know this world. And as a result of this sharp and quite dogmatic division he burdens himself with all the trouble of unreal and imaginary objects, and with the problem of error. I shall first state briefly the criticism of such a 'real world' from the point of view of *Appearance and Reality*, and elucidate it further by criticism of such analyses of the act of knowledge as those of Meinong and Messer.

There is a dilemma which may be said to be given at the start. Either the external world is presented always as it is, and is never more or other than what is given; or else there is a describable relation between our knowing and that which is known. And if we accept the first alternative, it is said, we are left with no real world at all, for anything and everything incongruous and inconsistent, will be equally real, and in no significant sense will it constitute a 'world'. We are then to assume one real world independent of our knowledge of it, surround consciousness with an opaque veil of 'subjectivity' and ask in what form and in what way reality penetrates this integument. We assume no acquaintance with objects except as presented, but the epistemologist makes it his task to prove that there is a relation between knowledge and its object which is not simply that of knowledge.

Mr Russell (*Mind*, 1904. 'Meinong's Theory of Complexes and Assumptions, III') gives a list of five theories of knowledge which is suggestive.

The Epistemologist's Theory of Knowledge

1. '[K]nowledge does not differ from what is known . . .
2. We may admit the distinction of content and object, but hold that the latter is merely immanent.
3. We may hold that the object is immanent when false, transcendent when true.
4. We may hold that when a judgment is false there is no object; but when true, there is a transcendent object.
5. We may hold that the object is always transcendent.'

The first of these is that which Mr Russell attributes to idealism, though to what idealism he refers I am unable to discover. I contend that every one of these accounts is ultimately meaningless, owing to the confusion of the practical with the metaphysical points of view. The last four all accept the distinction of content and object, though upon what grounds I am at a loss to say. 'When we consider the presentation of something simple, say redness, it is evident that the presentation and the object are distinct' (Russell, *ibid.*, p. 514). But in the first place (Chapter III, p. 62) it is not quite correct to say that redness is a presentation, and furthermore I cannot find any evidence offered for the distinctness of presentation and object. But (Russell, *ibid.*, p. 207): 'The content of a presentation exists when the presentation exists, but the object need not exist — it may be self-contradictory, it may be something which happens not to be a fact, such as a golden mountain, it may be essentially incapable of existence as for instance equality, it may be physical, not psychical, or it may be something which did exist or will exist, but does not exist at present. What is called the existence of an object in presentation is really not existence at all: it may be called pseudo-existence. . . . The content tends to be ignored in favour of the object; there are no natural designations for contents, which have to be named and distinguished by their objects.'

Such a theory of content and object is evidently based upon the assumption of a world of real and independent objects: it assumes that the typical case of apprehension is that of a physical object; it forces our apprehension of 'ideal' objects into the same mould, and it ends in the paradox that we may refer to an object when no object is present. It appears to assume also that there may be objects which are — in fact that the typical object is — merely existent, and do not to some extent subsist as well.

I wish to recall the criticism which I directed upon 'content' in the preceding chapter. From the argument there offered it would appear that the golden mountain is as real and objective as any thing else. If it were merely content the content would be the object, and we should have to account for our error in mistaking the one for the other. But it could not be even content unless it intended to be object. So far as the idea 'golden mountain' is a real idea, so far is it a real object. I will not however, pursue these comments farther until I have outlined the view of a 'real world' which these four theories mentioned by Mr Russell seem to over look. There is a real world, corresponding to that intended by these theories, which is neither identical with Bradley's Reality nor incompatible with it. And I may be at some pains to suggest what is essentially indefinable, what this real world is; why it is tempting as a starting-point for epistemology, why it is unreal inside a metaphysical system, yet presupposed by every system. I have agreed heartily to the views of Professor Alexander and Dr Nunn in regard to the reality of all objects. But it is evident that in practice this doctrine is hopelessly untrue. We are forced to assume that some objects are real and others simply unreal; it is only in refined practice that we find degree of reality to any extent useful, and we never, I think, dispense with the blunt 'real' and 'unreal' altogether. For without the unreal, as without the element of negation, you cannot have a world of finite experience at all. Such a world involves selection and emphasis, and we cannot too frequently be told that the world of practice is supported by interest and valuation. But our interests and our values, we shall be told vary from moment to moment. So does the real world, according to that fragment of it which happens to be the focus of our attention. Against the background of practical reality that is, are various systems both social and scientific, which are so to speak lived together in a coherence which cannot be formulated.

The Epistemologist's Theory of Knowledge

The process by which this world is constructed has of course two aspects. On the one hand the selection of certain experiences as real and the rejection of others builds up the world, and on the other hand the assumption of a real world gives a standard for such choice; the external world is thus doubly supported in its externality. Thus the distinction between that content which is merely personal and that which is objective is *not* a distinction between two classes of object absolutely, but a distinction valid only so long as we support one point of view — that of practical interest in the difference. There is a real world, if you like, which is full of contradictions, and it is our attempt to organize this world which gives the belief in a completely organized world, an hypothesis which we proceed to treat as an actuality — whence the question how and how far we come into contact with this world of absolute order.

The principle involved in the question of immanent and transcendent objects I believe to be this: a reality intended need not be in itself actual, though its actuality be presupposed in the reality of the intention. We intend, from our divers limited points of view, a single real world, and we forget that metaphysically this real world is only real so far as it finds realization through these points of view. It is not my purpose at this point to expound the doctrine of points of view, which will belong properly under the head of Solipsism, but only to sketch the outlines of the position from which Epistemology is criticized. I repeat then that the objective world is only actual in one or other point of view, but that each point of view intends to be, not a point of view, but the world one and impersonal, and in this double aspect, according to which reality is on the one hand given and on the other hand merely symbolized, I find what may be called in a way the transcendence of the object and the justification for the distinction between content and object. But it must be remarked that such a distinction has only practical validity, and does not hold where a particular content has not been already selected as real. It is not true to say that some objects are immanent and some transcendent by virtue of any characteristic which can be found in them *as*

90

objects, for all objects are equally immanent and equally transcendent. The criterion of reality, therefore, is to be found, not in the relation of the object to the subject, but in the directness with which the object is relatable to the |intended world — for it is not always the same sphere of reality to which we refer our objects. So that the reality of the object does not lie in the object itself, but in the extent of the relations which the object possesses without significant falsification of itself. These relations are all different points of view upon the object — i.e. they relate different aspects to a single point of reference: in this process of relation the object itself is altered, for what was at first the object pure and simple becomes the object under a single aspect. And a point of view, it may here be remarked, need not be considered as identical with one human consciousness; so that we may be said to move from one point of view to another when we determine an object by another relation. If this be true, then the movement between one 'finite centre' and another will not differ in kind from that inside of one consciousness, and will consist in the constitution of a real world by ideal references of many aspects.

In this case, the 'real world' of epistemology (to be distinguished from the Reality of metaphysics) will be an essentially indefinite world of identical references of an indefinite number of points of view, particularly those of other civilized adults with whom we come in contact, but quite possibly extending to all finite centres with which we can establish an identical reference. In the light of this view, and recalling the account of idea which I have laboured to express in the first three chapters several of the distinctions of Meinong appear to me elaborate superfluities. I would choose as an example his distinction of *Inhalt* (content) and *Gegenstand* (object) with reference to *Pseudoexistenz* (pseudo-existence). It is meaningless, Meinong says,* to speak of an object as existent only 'in der Vorstellung' ('in presentation'). 'An Object that exists only "in my presentation", simply does not exist at all . . .: We may now summarise as follows: existence, for the knower, is, viewed from the standpoint of the Object, a pseudo-

* *Erfahrungsgrundlagen unseres Wissens*, p. 56.

existence, and it remains only to establish what, in such cases, the actual existent is, which is thus in the strict sense perceived.' *We must clearly distinguish, he says, the *Inhalt* of a *Vorstellung* (presentation) from its *Gegenstand*. 'If I think first of red and then of green, it naturally cannot be the same, or a precisely similar presentation, whereby I first apprehend the one object and then the other. But that which respectively distinguishes these two presentations, so that the first is appropriated to the one object and the second to the other, is their content. Clearly, the object apprehended in a presentation cannot possibly exist; but still less, then, can the content, whereby it is apprehended. The latter is a constituent of the presentation, and cannot be absent, or the presentation itself would be absent too.'** A good deal depends, of course, on the use of the word *Vorstellung* and I have been unable to find — admitting, however, that I find Meinong an exceedingly difficult author — that the meaning of this very obscure word is anywhere defined; and I have occasion to complain, indeed, that just those words are taken for granted which have the most need of new or revised definitions. What, in the quotation just given, is the difference of *Vorstellung* but the difference of object? Both *Vorstellung* and *Inhalt* seem here identical with object. For the 'idea' here in question is not a logical idea, not the idea which we predicate of reality; the idea in this sense would be for Meinong identical with the object, since there is no question of predicating the *Vorstellung* of red of the real red. The idea here is the psychologist's idea, which is for the psychologist an aspect of the object

* '[E]in Objekt, das nur "in meiner Vostellung" existiert, eigentlich gar nicht existiert . . . : Man kann jetzt kurz sagen: die Existenz, die er erkennt, ist, vom Standpunkte der Objekte besehen, eine Pseudoexistenz, und es bleibt nur festzustellen, was in solchen Fällen das wirklich Existente, das also im strengen Sinne Wahrgenommene ist.'
** 'Denke ich das eine Mal an Rot das andere Mal an Grün, so kann es natürlich nicht dieselbe resp. eine genau gleiche Vorstellung sein, vermöge deren ich einmal diesen, einmal jenen Gegenstand erfasse. Das aber, worin diese beiden Vorstellungen jedenfalls verschieden sind, wodurch die eine diesem, die andere jenem Gegenstande zugeordnet ist, das ist ihr Inhalt. Bekanntlich muss der Gegenstand, den eine Vorstellung erfasst, durchaus nicht existieren; um so gewisser aber der Inhalt, durch den sie ihn erfasst. Er ist ein Stück an der Vorstellung, das nicht fehlen kann, ohne das die Vorstellung selbst fehlt.' (*ibid.*, 57.)

in mental context. I have already protested against amputating this aspect for the purpose of a 'special science'; but to graft the member on again after it is dead seems to me even more gratuitous. In the sense in which there are two ideas (red and green) there are not at the same time two objects, for we have substituted the ideas for the objects. And when we proceed to talk of the 'content' of an idea we are simply making a devious return to the object. It is not true, I have contended, to say that an idea has an object, for idea *is* (not *has*) a reference to an object. So far as the idea is real it is the object, so far as the idea is unreal the object is unreal or indeterminate.

The distinction between idea and content of idea may be accounted for perhaps in connection with Meinong's analysis of *Ausdruck* (expression) and *Bedeutung* (meaning).* 'Thus anyone who utters, say, the word "sun", normally gives *expression* also, whether he wants to or not, to the fact that a certain presentation, either of perception or imagination, is occurring in him. The nature of this presentation is determined initially by what is presented therein, namely its object, and this object is in fact what is meant by the word "sun".'**

It would appear from this passage that we express the idea, but mean the object. This being admitted, it is well to ask whether the object, in the case of an unreal object, is merely the content of the idea: and we find, I think, the psychologist's error of treating two points of view as if they were one. The idea in question refers merely to the judgment made by the hearer to the effect that the speaker has 'an idea of' certain objects; but the object apprehended by the hearer is an object which from the point of view of the speaker does not exist. The speaker can only mean; and even if he means his own 'state of consciousness' what is really active is a meaning which is not meant. The idea, furthermore, which is

* See *U. Annahmen, 2te Aufl.*, p. 24 ff.
** 'Wer also etwa das Wort "Sonne" ausspricht, bringt dadurch normaler-weise, gleichviel ob er es auch will oder nicht, zum *Ausdruck*, dass sich eine bestimmte Vorstellung, es kann natürlich so gut Wahrnehmung's wie Einbildungs-vorstellung sein, in ihm zuträgt. Was für eine Vostellung das ist, bestimmt sich zunächst nach dem, was durch vorgestellt wird, also ihrem Gegenstande, und dieser Gegenstand ist eben das, was das Wort "Sonne" bedeutet.' (*ibid.*, 25.)

apprehended is only a half-object: it exists, that is, as an object only by our half putting ourselves in the place of the speaker and half contemplating him as an object. The distinction, consequently, between *Ausdruck* and *Bedeutung* must[31] be drawn too closely. For no expression is even expression unless we attribute it meaning, and meaning cannot be merely contemplated, but must be *erlebt* (experienced). Hence even in the case of error — Pseudoexistenz — the object must be transcendent or there is no object at all: and in this I am in accord with Mr Russell.

The occasion for the distinction of immanent and transcendent objects is obviously the fact of error. No object can, we find, be merely immanent, for the reason that so far as an object is an object it will have relations which transcend it, transcend the perception; relations which constitute it, but which ultimately transform and absorb it. The poorer an object is in relations, the less it is object; and the limiting case of pseudoexistence is an object with no relations — this would be the only purely imaginary object, and would of course not be an object at all, but a feeling, which as such, would have its relations of another sort. Mr Russell's declaration that all objects are transcendent, however seems to provoke only new difficulties. (p. 515)[32]: 'It is not maintained, of course, that the object must *exist*; that would be to maintain that a certain specific proposition must hold of the object, whereas all that seems essential is that there should *be* such an object; and the assertion of being, if not analytic, is yet more nearly so than any other assertion.' The content, Mr Russell tells us, implies the object and the relation of the content to object. This seems very much like my theorem (p. 90), that a reality intended need not be itself actual though its reality be presupposed in the reality of the intention, but it leaves to the transcendence of the object, as Mr Russell states it, only a formal value, through its insinuation of the distinction between existence and being; a distinction which implies that Mr Russell means no more by transcendence than Meinong does by immanence. So that Mr Russell's theory appears to end in bankruptcy, inasmuch as we are left without a criterion for either truth or judgment or reality of object.

Meinong's theory of perception is complicated, as I suggested above, by the division which he draws between real and ideal objects, between *inferiora* and *superiora*. Mr Russell classifies *superiora* as follows: relations (including likeness, differences, and the complexes formed of terms related by a relation), and the kind of objects (which we may call plurals) of which numbers other than 0 and 1 can be asserted. The difficulty which I find with this account is that it would seem possible for virtually any object to be either inferior or superior: a melody, for example is superior and composed of tones as its *inferiora*; but the simple tone is composed of vibrations, and is in fact as absolutely a 'zeitverteiltes Gegenstand' as is the melody. Furthermore, it is by no means clear what the relation of a *superius* to its *inferiora* is. A melody, as Mr Russell observes, is not a fifth note; what is added is the relation — but 'rightly related' to the constituents! Now it may be asked whether a relation to its terms, whether the relations is apprehended as an object in the same way as the object, and whether in any complex there are two *superiora*, the relation uniting, and the whole complex.[33] And finally I would ask (and this is the only essential question) whether the division really corresponds to the objects with which we actually come into contact.

It is only with great trepidation that I venture to interpret so obscure an author as Alexis von Meinong. But I am interested to note my own impression that the ideal object (which is always an object of higher order) tends to the foreground of certainty, while the real object drops into the obscurity of a noumenon. So, toward the end of the book *Über die Erfahrungsgrundlagen (On the Empirical Foundations of Our Knowledge)* the author is apparently more and more cautious in attributing characters to the real object. (P. 93): The object O is divided into o ('das Dingmoment', the factor of thinghood) and o' ('die Gesamtheit der "im äusseren Aspekte gegebenen Eigenschaften"',' the totality of characteristics presented to outward view). 'In respect of o, the chalk is hardly to be distinguished from the inkstand; to be sure, the perceptual presentation of the former offers us one o' for the purpose, and that of the latter another: but these are precisely those sensible qualities, for whose real presence we have no evidence.' (*Ibid.*, p. 94): 'The phenomenal determinations o_1' and o_2' are paralleled, in fact, by noumenal determinations $\bar{o}_1$ and $\bar{o}_2$, of which it is evident, indeed, that the very same relations of comparison hold between them as between the o's; wherein lies implicit at the same time a claim in any case self-evident, namely that the substantial factor o, guaranteed to us by the good evidence already validated, does not exist, as it were, in unnatural or indeed impossible, isolation, but that the existent does in fact consist of things having characteristics.'*

This is, if you like, knowledge of an external reality, but it is knowledge of a very critical sort indeed. The *superiora* become *Erkenntnisinstrument* ('instruments of knowledge'), and while the 'aspects' furnish evidence, not for themselves but for the objects (or perceptions?) of which they are aspects, yet it is the aspect which is presented. The thing is known, but only through appearances which exist as references to the thing, and do not necessarily give evidence for their own existence. This seems to me essentially the position of the critical philosophy: the thing is known through its appearances, but as soon as the distinction is made appearance and thing fall apart, and appearance replaces thing as a point of attention.

The distinction between inferior and superior objects, on the whole, strikes me as thoroughly critical. To treat things, not as moments of objectivity, but as ultimate lumps which can be

---

* 'Die Kreide unterscheidet sich vom Tintenfass schwerlich in betreff des o dafür bietet uns die Wahrnehmungsvorstellung der ersteren freilich ein o_1', di des letzteren ein o_2': aber das sind ja eben jene sensiblen Qualitäten, für dere Dasein wir keine Evidenz haben.' (p. 94): 'Den phänomenalen Bestimmunge o_1', o_2 etc. stehen vielmehr noumenale Bestimmungen $\bar{o}_1$, $\bar{o}_2$ etc. gegenübe von denen eben evident ist, dass zwischen ihnen die nämlichen Vergleichung relationen gelten wie zwischen den o', worin zugleich die allerdings selbstver ständliche Behauptung beschlossen liegt, dass das substantielle Moment o, da uns durch die bereits geltend gemachte gute Evidenz gesichert ist, nicht etwa i unnatürlicher oder eigentlich unmöglicher Isoliertheit existiert, sondern dass d Existierende doch jedenfalls Dinge mit Eigenschaften sind.'

grasped after all relations* have been stripped away, seems to be the attempt of both Meinong and Kant. To treat ideal relations as 'superior' objects, somehow built upon the real objects, and in a sense dependent upon them (Russell, *op. cit.*, p. 207 ff.)[34] is a step toward making relations into categories. For it appears (unless I misinterpret) that the ideal relations are more certainly known than the real, being (in Meinong's sense) *a priori*, and the objects of 'inner perception' are more certainly known than those of outer perception. (*Op. cit.*, p. 99)[35]: 'Thus in dealing with ideal objects, there is no need at all to disclaim the influence of subjectivity; but so far as the evidence is not still to seek, this leads merely to a sort of selection among the equally available *superiora*, whose totality the intrinsically limited intellect cannot attempt to assess. But this subjectivity in no way compromises the validity of what we are able to know *a priori*, once we obtain it. Thus things-in-themselves are like, unlike, etc.'**

But it would appear that this likeness among objects is a matter of inference and not of direct acquaintance. We do not know reality in substance, we know it in relation: we know, that is, a relation among content which cannot be falsified when carried over to the thing, inasmuch as the content is only content with reference to the thing, so that the relation is not directly known of the content as such. The profoundest obscurity enfolds the notion of *Adäquatheit* (adequateness), an ideal relation between the object of the idea and reality (*Annahmen*, p. 263). If *Wirklichkeit* (actuality) is real, then in the apprehension of an ideal object (cf. *ibid.*, p. 265) I do not see what the relation of *Adäquatheit* between the ideal object apprehended and the 'real' ideal object can be, for there cannot be two sets of ideal objects,

* 'For a thing to exist it must possess identity. . . . and further, this identity is ideal.' *Appearance*, p. 61.

** 'So wird man in betreff idealer Gegenstände den Einfluss der Subjectivität durchaus nicht in Abrede zu stellen brauchen; diese führt aber, soweit die Evidenz nicht ausbleibt, nur zu einer Art Auswahl unter den gleichsam verfügbaren Superioren, deren Gesamtheit der durch seine Natur begrentzte Intellekt zu ermessen gar nicht versuchen kann. Aber die Gültigkeit dessen, was wir, so wie wir einmal beschaffen sind, a priori zu erkennen vermögen, wird durch diese Subjectivität in keiner Weise in Frage gestellt. Die Dinge an sich sind also gleich, ungleich etc.'

and the ideal relation between the ideal object apprehended and the real object can be nothing more than a relation of identity. In this case the *Adäquatheit* must be between the real content of an idea and a real complex, which would mean that in knowledge we do not apprehend relations but a specific case of relation, and that the complex of terms related is not ideal but real, and that the relation of aspect to thing is always a real relation.

We are here in full cry after the familiar *ignis fatuus* of epistemology, the search for terms, which persist in dissolving into relations. The reliance upon 'inner perception' is I think only another case of retreat to a relation as more secure than a thing. It is evidently the conclusion of the preceding chapter that there is properly no such thing as internal perception, and that in any case it provides no more certain knowledge than outer perception, but perhaps less, and certainly later. There is surely no more evidence in memory* than in perception, whether it be the memory of a feeling, desire, or perception. To pass from the subject to the content of a perception is not in general to pass from the less to the more certain. For as we have seen, every perception has an object, and whether that object is 'real' or not depends simply on the number and kind of relations which, in a particular context, we may for practical purposes demand: reality is a convention. To fall back on the content is simply to assert a quasi-object: there was an experience, as if. . . . To make an object of the content is to attend to something quite as uncertain in evidence as any other object. The content objectified, that is, is something which was never as such experienced; because the I which attends to the content is a wider, more developed I than the I which first experienced the content. So that the content is not in any exact sense a part of the self, and is subject to exactly the same conditions of evidence as any other object. There will be, then, evidence for object and evidence for content, but not necessarily

* Bradley, *Mind*, April 1899, p. 160: 'Our justification for regarding memory as in general accurate is briefly this, that by taking such a course we are best able to order and harmonize our world. There is in the end no other actual or possible criterion of fact and truth, and the search for a final fact and for an absolute datum is everywhere the pursuit of a mere *ignis fatuus*.'

stronger for one than for the other, and in most cases, I am inclined to believe, stronger for object than for content.

I have already raised objections to the drawing and quartering of reality into real and ideal objects: this objection I should now like to amplify. I seem to find here some confusion as to just what is implied by the word *object*: and I cannot but feel that the distinction of real and ideal, inferior and superior objects, is a clumsy substitute for the notion of degrees of truth and reality. It is admitted (Russell, *op. cit.*, p. 352)[36] that the division between objects and objectives is not altogether sharp (cf. 'black-board' and 'the blackness of the board'). May we not then fairly inquire whether there can be found a single case of an object which cannot be treated as an objective? or indeed of an objective which cannot be treated as an object? Even the perception of the familiar epistemologist's table can be treated as the assertion *that* certain experiences are given — the table being only the condensed aspect of the objective asserted. And as Meinong affirms that a perception is also an *Existenzurteil* (existential judgment), so any judgment involves as well the perception of the judgment (i.e., the perception of its correctness).

The object has not yet been exactly defined. An object is as such a point of attention, and thus anything and everything to which we may be said to direct attention is an object.

But the objects among which we live are much more than this; here we have abstracted from everything about a thing which could localize it either in a 'subjective' or in an 'objective' world. The element of objectivity is the capacity of anything to be, or to be considered as (the distinction will explain itself later) a point of attention, but the point of attention is of course only an abstraction. It is only as the point of attention becomes qualified — becomes a *what* — that it is even a *that*; a number of characteristics, none of which is essential to its objectivity, and none of which is objective in the sense of being an object, nevertheless constitute *its* objectivity: its *thatness* is in direct ratio to its *whatness*. And the thing, in order to be a thing even, must be capable of entering into a kind of existence in which it is not a thing. I do not argue that a thing ceases to be a thing when it ceases to be a point of attention: this is I believe supposed to be the point of view of subjective idealism. For I do not recognize the validity of the question. There is an identity which persists, an identity due to which the objectivity is not annihilated, but rendered meaningless. The thing does not cease to exist, it exists in other ways, ways which are not thinghood, but can only be expressed or suggested in terms of thinghood. And without the potentiality of these other forms of existence the thing would not even be a thing: *existence*, I mean to say, *is not identical with thinghood*. The world is not made up of things, nor of things and 'other things'; but existence is capable of appearing more or less under the aspect of thinghood. The account which I offer is, I know, anything but lucid! I can only plead in excuse that the point is one of the most difficult in the theory of knowledge. But one of the consequences, which will perhaps go to make the matter more intelligible, is that there are no objects of strictly lower order, and no objects of strictly higher order. What Meinong has in mind are two aspects of existence which when contemplated, are both objects, but so far as they are objects, are of the same order. The only alternative, I insist, is to assume that the lower objects alone are objects, and the higher, categories, that only 'real' things exist, and that in point of fact there are no real things, but only things in themselves, i.e. hypothetical limits. And from this point of view Meinong has, as I intimated, only a step to take to Kant.

The whole question is, as Mr Russell suggests, closely bound up with the theory of time. Meinong maintains that the objects of lower order may be directly perceived. But it is surely evident that so far as an object has meaning it is not an object of this sort. For meaning involves relations; at least (we need) the relation of identity* through which a universality of function is recognized through a diversity of situation.

* 'For a thing to exist it must possess identity; and identity seems a possession with a character at best doubtful. If it is merely ideal, the thing itself can hardly be real. . . . And this identical content is called ideal because it transcends given existence. Existence is given only in presentation, and, on the other hand, the thing is a thing only if its existence goes beyond the now, and extends into the past. *Appearance*, pp. 61–2.

The Epistemologist's Theory of Knowledge

And I do not see how you can make the distinction between *superiora* and *inferiora* at all unless you claim the existence and the perceptibility of *inferiora* apart from *superiora*. Surely the whole construction falls to the ground once you admit their inseparability. For in this case there not only is no logical priority, but the one is so dependent for its existence upon the other that the two are only discriminated aspects of the same moment of objectivity, and we may say that in a sense neither of the two is the object we know.

The 'object which we know' is however only a certain aspect. We encounter a difficulty in the fact that we are forced to use the same term 'object' for more than one aspect. For it is clear that the slightest consideration of the nature of an object analyses ideal from real elements. Any description must bring to light elements which subsist rather than exist, and some elements are chosen as existents simply with reference to others that do not: none can be said to be in itself purely existent. You cannot get a world of real things by joining together a number of subsistents with a number of existents, for it turns out that there is nothing in the world which is wholly in time — there are, that is, no pure *thats*. No object, it is implied, is merely an object; for the real presence of ideal elements in the simplest and most objective of objects implies a kinship between that object and all other objects in which that idea element is exemplified; the mere identity of an object with itself constitutes a relation between that object and all other objects. So that the curious dualism of Mr Russell (*Problems*, pp. 99–100) which has much in common with obvious, though I can hardly think correct, interpretations of Plato, will not hold good of a world which is always partially in time, but never wholly in time, with respect to any of its elements.

What constitutes a real object, accordingly, is the practical need or occasion. We may treat, that is, an object of attention as a term or as a complex as occasion demands, and it is only a question of practice to what point, under analysis, it remains the same object. And it will always be a question on your hands just what it is that persists in time. Ordinarily there is no difficulty, for the object is not *bestimmt*; it fluctuates as occasion demands, and as elements in it are treated as real or as ideal, but as the terms are analysed into relations, it appears finally that nothing is in time except time itself. This point of view, however, is of course only a limit, and is never reached.

So much for the 'existence' of 'real' objects. It will be said on the other side that there are objects which are purely ideal: relations, such as identity and difference, and the objects of pure mathematics. To this also I must object. We *intend* ideal objects, just as we *intend* real ones, and in practice the difference in intention is difference in reality. But I do not see how, in a critical examination of first principles, such a distinction can maintain itself absolutely. The objection is as follows. The existent and the subsistent are two aspects of reality which are intended but never actually grasped, and the difference between them is not the difference between two classes of object, for *in so far as* they are objects they are of the same sort; the difference is *extra-objective*. What for example do we attend to when we make an object of the relation 'difference'. So far as it is an object, it is not a relation; it is something corresponding to that relation in the world of objects: not as a correspondence of two separate entities, but by continuous transition. And this *object* is subject to all the difficulties of the existent object in reversed order. As a relation it is a relation of terms; as an object it is a simple term or a complex of terms again related. It will not do to say that the relation is apprehended in a case of itself; that the relation difference is grasped through the difference of a specific content, red and green. For this is to admit that the true object is the complex (*a*) red-different-from-green, or (*b*) difference-of green-from-red. (*a*) and (*b*) are evidently the same object in one sense and different objects in another. The practical attention is in the same direction, but there is a difference of emphasis: one cannot say absolutely that the objects are the same. So far as we regard it as the same (*a*) will represent the tendency in the direction of existence, and (*b*) the tendency in the direction of subsistence: but red-and-green on the one hand and difference on the other will never be actualized. We do not need to refute the protest that difference is not different, and that whiteness is not white, in order to reach this conclusion. For we mean only that neither subsistence nor existence can be real, and that what is intended in the act of attending to an object is always something real.

The last point needs some elucidation. An abstraction, it is here argued, is not merely *as such* an object of attention. The abstraction has an individual existence, though not independent of that from which it is abstracted, and it is this individual existence which is the object so far as there is an object. If there is given in primary experience a real object A from which we abstract the superior ideal object a, then a is at once something more and something less than A. It is less in that it is intended to be merely a subsistent aspect of A, and more in that it has an existence of its own, with conditions to a large degree independent of A. And in this way it is also in a sense less than itself, in that being a subsistent, it is limited as well by conditions of existence. This leads to the consideration of the relation of symbol to that which it symbolizes.*

I mean here by symbol both what Mr Peirce calls by that name and what he calls an eicon; excluding the index.[37] Symbol, I mean, in the sense of the real (or rather objective) end of a continuity which terminates at one end in an *intended existent* or *subsistent* and at the other end in an object (*erfassbar*, apprehensible) which must have both existent and subsistent aspects. Now in any use of a word which symbolizes an abstraction the actual object of attention, I submit, is exceedingly variable: there is not simply one determinate object in various contexts, but the object varies with the context. Thus, in any use of an abstract term, we may distinguish between the logical meaning, which is an intended object, and the real meaning, which is a part of the experience and not an object real or intended. For the intended object we always substitute to

---

* 'No abstraction (whatever its origin) is in the end defensible. For they are none of them quite true, and with each the amount of possible error must remain unknown. The truth asserted is not, and cannot be, taken as real by itself. The background is ignored because it is assumed to make no difference ... But an assumption of this kind obviously goes beyond our knowledge.' *Appearance*, p. 478.

perhaps a greater or a less degree the present symbol. It must be emphasized, however, that there is properly speaking, no relation between the symbol and that which it symbolizes, because they are continuous. The reality without the symbol would never be known, and we cannot say that it would even exist (or subsist); but on the other hand the symbol furnishes proof of the reality, inasmuch as without the reality it would not be that symbol: i.e. there would be an identity left which would for our purposes be irrelevant. The word 'relation' would not be the word 'relation' without the reality 'relation' which is not in itself an object; for no word can exist without a meaning, and if the word 'relation' did not have the meaning 'relation' it would have to have some other meaning. You cannot, that is to say, determine two realities, the word and its meaning: the word (here the existent) is continuous with the meaning (here subsistent). It consequently transpires that neither the word alone (for there is no word alone) is the object, for the logical meaning (which is an abstraction and cannot be grasped without the word) nor the total of word and meaning, for there is no total; word and meaning being continuous, and the continuity not an object.*[38]

The (true) object, then, is never a mere universal, nor a mere particular, nor a complex composed of universals and particulars. It was known, I should suppose, by Plato, that universals and particulars cannot be in any meaningful sense related, inasmuch as they are not separate existences. And so I cannot find any more satisfaction in the account of Mr Russell than in that of Meinong.

---

* The following passage appears to have some appropriateness: 'We must attach *some* meaning to the words we use, if we are to speak significantly and not utter mere noise; and the meaning we attach to our words must be something with which we are acquainted. Thus when, for example, we make a statement about Julius Caesar, it is plain that Julius Caesar himself is not before our minds, since we are not acquainted with him. We have in mind some *description* of Julius Caesar: . . . "the founder of the Roman Empire", or, perhaps, merely "the man whose name was *Julius Caesar*". (In this last description, *Julius Caesar* is a noise or shape with which we are acquainted.) Thus our statement does not mean quite what it seems to mean, but means something involving, instead of Julius Caesar, some description of him composed wholly of particulars and universals with which we are acquainted.' Russell, *Problems*, pp. 58–9. But I find the notion of acquaintance completely unsatisfactory.

For Mr Russell, as for Meinong, universals or particulars may be known by direct acquaintance. But whereas for Meinong both seem to be treated as direct objects, Russell's acquaintance certainly refers to another kind of knowledge than that of objects. Thus acquaintance is defined as 'direct cognitive relation to that object. . . .'* The cognitive relation here is presentation. Sense-data, universals, and perhaps the self are thus known. Now whatever may be said of universals, neither sense-data nor the self are known primitively by what is commonly called presentation, i.e. presentation as an object: for we are surely somehow 'acquainted' with sense-data and the self in the practical apprehensions of objects long before we make objects (presentations) of the sense-data themselves.

The theory of Meinong starts from the postulate of the reality of objects — everything that is real is an object. Mr Russell starts apparently from the reality of universals and sense-data, and from these elements late in the order of knowledge** he builds up the external world. 'We have acquaintance', says Mr Russell, in a passage which strikingly recalls Locke (*Problems*, pp. 51–2), 'in sensation with the data of the outer senses,*** and in introspection with the data of what may be called the inner sense — thoughts, feelings, desires, etc. . . . In addition to our acquaintance with particular existing things, we also have acquaintance with what we shall call *universals*, that is to say, general ideas, such as *whiteness, diversity, brotherhood*, and so on.' Inasmuch as we are stated (*Ibid.*, 52) not to be acquainted with physical objects it may be inferred that we are not acquainted with anything in its character of *object*, but only in the felt whole of experience; with the interesting consequence that objects are not directly known but inferred, and that anything which is named is so far not

---

* 'Knowledge by Acquaintance and Knowledge by Description', *Proc. Arist. Soc.*, 1910–11.

** Cf. '. . . [L]a mentalité des sociétés inférieures . . . comporte bien des représentations abstraites, et des représentations générales; mais ni cette abstraction, ni cette généralité ne sont celles de nos concepts.' Lévy-Bryhl, *Les Fonctions Mentales*, p. 137.

*** Cf. Nettleship, *Remains*, I, pp. 176–7.

among our acquaintance. And here again we encounter an interesting rapprochement of realism to Kantianism. The entities (to use as non-committal a term as possible) which we know (by acquaintance) are not objects but means by which we apprehend objects, while the object is directly quite beyond the span of our knowledge. There are, on this interpretation, 'no such things' as objects, there are only experiences. 'All names of places — London, England, Europe, the Earth, the Solar System — similarly involve, when used, descriptions which start from some one or more particulars with which we are acquainted. I suspect that even the Universe, as considered by metaphysics, involves such a connection with particulars.* In logic, on the contrary, where we are concerned not merely with what does exist, but with whatever might or could exist or be, no reference to actual particulars is involved.' (*Problems*, p. 56). In making a statement about something known only by description, Mr Russell says, we may *intend* to make the statements about the *object* itself — but we never do so (*ibid.*, p. 56). To know an object is simply to know that there is that object: we know only an objective which asserts an existence; and to say that we have direct acquaintance with that objective is not to make the object any more real.

Apparently another person may be an intended object, but can be a real object only to the person himself — and a person is not an object to himself, because he is directly acquainted with himself, and acquaintance is not a subject-object relation.** The world thus appears as an ideal construction of descriptions linked to the physiological and to the logical system.

What then is the relation of universals and particulars in the world of objects? 'A thing, of the every-day sort is constituted by a bundle of sensible qualities belonging to various senses, but sup-

* Cf. the idealistic doctrine of the essential connection of the universe with the moment of perception.

** It is true that in the article cited on page 105, acquaintance is defined as 'direct cognitive relation to that object.' But the whole account of acquaintance, both in this article and in the *Problems* seems to me to point directly to enjoyment and not to contemplation, and I cannot help feeling that one of the obscurities of Mr Russell's position lies in treating as objects what are at the same time meant not to be objects.

posed all to co-exist in one continuous portion of space.'* It is
apparently by a sort of projection of sense-data (not, it must be
remembered, themselves objects) that we obtain the reality (or
the illusion?) of a thing. This is, incidentally, very near to
Berkeley, nearer certainly than Mr Russell's interpretation of
Berkeley.** But it is, from a slightly different point of view, very
near to Kant. You have the data of sense united by logic, and
this determination of the manifold is for a subject, since the data
of sense are real only in acquaintance, and acquaintance means
the enjoyment by a subject. It would appear that the thing,
which is always an object of higher order (as there are properly
no objects of lower order for Mr Russell) is a logical construction,
composed of two sorts of material, sense-data and universals,
both of which are if you like objective, but hardly objective in the
same sense in which objects are objective. Consequently, on this
interpretation of Mr Russell's theory, one cannot say with
Meinong that objects are either existent or subsistent, or are
compounds of both ingredients, for the only entities which are
purely existent are those of sense and introspection, and the only
entities which are purely subsistent are universals.***

It is interesting to note, furthermore, how uncertain the
evidence for the existence of objects becomes when we begin by
assuming them absolutely, and on this theory. The only things
that we know by acquaintance 'are neither true nor false': sense-
data (*Problems*, p. 113), universals, and the objects of inner
perception.**** The latter, as I intimated, are so far as known by

* 'Relations of Universals and Particulars', *Proc. Arist. Soc.*, 1911–12, pp. 6–7.

** Cf. 'The ideas of sight and touch make two species, entirely distinct and
heterogeneous'.... (*Prin. of Human Knowledge*, XLIV) with 'If we talk of *one*
space we substitute for the perceived sense data a collection of pieces of matter
having whatever qualities the science of the moment may prescribe.' 'Universals
and Particulars', p. 7.[39]

*** It is true that Mr Russell speaks elsewhere as if we were directly acquainted
with things. (*Problems*, p. 136): '[we may know] ... by means of *acquaintance*
with the complex fact itself, which may (in a large sense) be called perception,
though it is by no means confined to objects of the senses.' But I do not see how,
according to the passage quoted earlier, we can be directly acquainted with
anything that is strictly true or false of the real world.

**** Cf. Locke's Essay, Bk. II, Ch. I, Para. 19, 'Consciousness is the perception
of what passes in a man's own mind.'

acquaintance not objects — so far as they are objects they are subject to all the conditions of outer perceptions. The universals also are assuredly neither true nor false, inasmuch as you do not have falsehood without an existence proposition.

Whiteness and brotherhood are it is true *a priori* (in the sense defined by Meinong, which is ultimately the sense of Kant as well) but they are not knowledge, nor are they known. We *experience* universals, and we *experience* particulars, but knowledge is always of *objects*, in which both are elements. And this is as true of the objects of mathematics, I submit, as of anything else: the actual object is always composed of existent and of subsistent elements, and is defined (practically) as an existent or as a subsistent object by the tendency of its use. Numbers, considered as merely subsistent, have no true or false combinations, for they are not known. They are simply *erlebt* (experienced) in the contemplation of objects to which they apply; 2 plus 2=4 is thus neither true nor false; but when we add four real objects together, we know (as objects), that two of the objects with two of the objects makes four objects, and we experience by acquaintance the 2 plus 2=4. We can of course abstract the numbers simply and determine them by a moment of objectivity; but what we have then is not the number in itself but an object corresponding to it. For how should objects apply to objects, as numbers apply to things? Numbers are not objects; nor, as I shall try to point out later, is number strictly a category.

The question then from the point of view of Mr Russell's philosophy, is how we proceed from acquaintance with entities which are neither real nor unreal to a knowledge of real objects which is true or false. 'We agreed provisionally that physical objects cannot be quite like our sense-data, but may be regarded as *causing* our sensations' (*Problems*, p. 30). Space, moreover, is an *assumption* (*ibid.*, pp. 30, 31). Time consists in an order of before and after, but we cannot apparently be sure that the time-order which events seem to have is the same as the time-order which they do have (*ibid.*, p. 32). In regard to the characters of objects, secondary qualities are not characters of physical objects (*ibid.*, p. 35), but in an experience of red and blue, we may 'reasonably presume' (*ibid.*, p. 34) that a difference in the object corresponds to the difference of red and blue. 'Thus we find that, although the *relations* of physical objects have all sorts of knowable properties, derived from their correspondence with the relations of sense-data, the physical objects themselves remain unknown in their intrinsic nature, so far at least as can be discovered by means of the senses' (*ibid.*, p. 34). This seems very near to *Funktionsbegriff* (functional conception). The thing, if it *is* any more than a function of these relations is the merest assumption of popular prejudice. And these difficulties of a dualistic realism come from the standpoint of epistemology — of assuming that there is a real world outside of our knowledge and asking how we may know it.

Another difficulty of this point of view is the problem of time in knowledge and in reality. Knowledge of a universal, if a universal could be an object, would be knowledge of an object which is not in time, and the knowledge consequently would be out of time. For we attend to something, and if our attention is a temporal process the object can hardly fail to persist in time. But on the other hand, if existent objects are wholly in time, the very persistence of our attention upon them will involve the holding together of various moments of sensation by a common meaning, and that meaning will not be within the time to which it refers. I have tried to indicate one way of escape from this dilemma, in asserting the relativity of the subsistent and the existent, and pointing out the fact that a real object always has existent and subsistent elements. And this is substantially the conclusion of Mr Russell from one point of view, if as several passages imply the object is a sort of projection composed of universals and particulars known by acquaintance. But there is a further difficulty in the apprehension of these composite entities: 'And as with space, the qualitative content — which is not merely temporal, and apart from which the terms related would have no character — presents an insoluble problem. How to combine this in unity with the time which it fills, and again how to establish each aspect apart, are both beyond our resources. And time so far, like space, has turned out to be appearance.' (*Appearance* p. 34).

Just what is the meaning of simultaneity of perceiving and perceived? When I perceive an object, is there any meaning in the statement that the object is 'there' at the same time that my perception is 'there'? If we make this assertion, and affirm that the object is composed of sense-data which are strictly in time and universals (relations) which are not in time, we face the question: what time is it that the object exists in? 'It must not be supposed', says Mr Russell, 'that the various states of different physical objects have the same time-order as the sense-data which constitute the perceptions of those objects' (*Problems*, p. 33). We thus have two time-orders which are not reducible to each other, or the possibility of a continuum of various time-orders from the immediate order of experience *sensa* to the object itself, which, so far as it is *that* object, is not in time at all. And reality seems to fluctuate between these two impossible limits. Impossible, because on the one hand that which is purely in time cannot be said to exist at all. To exist it must be a *what*, and to be a *what* is to have (internal) ideal relations to other *whats*, relations which are not in time. And on the other hand, the object of perception cannot be consistent with itself as an object, because so far as it is that object, it is timeless; and so far as it changes, it never was that object, but a remoter object which is capable of persisting through the two states of itself: any object which is wholly real is independent of time, and after any noticed change that which it was previously is to be regarded as an appearance. The time-order then will vary according to what we take as the object — the 'real' sun, for example, or the perceived sun. The two are, if you like, the same sense-data in different relations, and for two objects to exist at the same time means an alliance by the same ideal relation. What does it mean to say that my character and the ten o'clock train, or the reputation of Herbert Spencer and his volume which lies on my table, or my table and the electrons exist at the same time? There is no exact meaning, and the statement has meaning only so far as we refer both to a single world, in which we vaguely feel that they are reconciled by experience; they are held together, that is, by a feeling of their *identical reference*, though that to which they refer does not exist.

This explanation (if it deserve the name) is the only escape that I can find from the time difficulty in perception. There is no time difficulty, because perception isn't in time; but there are several time-orders, and the collision occurs only when we arbitrarily assume that one is real and that there is a separate order of perception which must somehow correspond to it. But in a dualistic realism, the time difficulty appears very serious indeed, and real time seems to be as much an inference as is real space. So here again I suspect that we approach very close to criticism. For the real time and real space are demanded only by the way the problem has been set: a real (physical) world is assumed, then when we come to ask how we know this world, it appears that all we are sure of is certain data and forms of immediate experience, out of which the physical world is constructed — as a consequence of which the 'objectivity' of the external world becomes otiose or meaningless.

CHAPTER V

The Epistemologist's Theory of Knowledge

continued

I should now like to discuss some points in connection with unreal objects, and the theories of Meinong and Russell, indicating the realistic assumptions which underlie their solutions, and which alone create the problem. This will serve as an introduction to the larger question of denoting, meaning and context.

There are two questions here involved: that of the existence of unreal objects, and that of the truth or falsity of statements about unreal objects. And again, in the case of unreal objects, there are objects of hallucination, objects of imagination, and objects denoted, but apparently neither believed in nor assumed (the round square). It is chiefly with the last that these two authors are engaged. With regard to all of these types of object I would recall what I have said of the relations of real and ideal, and would urge the following contention: the problem is wholly factitious, and owes its origin to the false assumption of epistemology — the assumption that there is one world of external reality which is consistent and complete: an assumption which is not only ungrounded but in some sense certainly false. Reality contains irreducible contradictions and irreconcilable points of view. How this statement is consistent with a monistic metaphysic I shall endeavour to show in another place.

I wish to touch upon the facts of visual hallucination first, because, while the problem is essentially the same as that dealt with by Meinong and Russell, it appears in a more readily apprehensible form, and because it has by some been reduced to a different explanation from that of unreal objects in judgment, whereas I believe the hallucination to be in virtually the same position as the round square; both are non-existent, and both are intended objects. Both assert their reality, though perhaps in a difference of degree. Professor Holt says (*The New Realism*, p. 306) in stating the claim of an hypothetical opponent: '. . . not the distorted image as such, but the distorted image which *asserts itself to be*, or which *the realist asserts to be the real object* — . . . this is the crux for realism.' This appears to involve a *petitio principii*: it is not admitted that there is a 'distorted image as such'. In the case of the stick in water (which is quite distinct from the phenomena of hallucination) there is if you please 'distorted image as such'; if, that is, you abstract the stick under normal conditions and choose to call that the stick. But here you have only a case of completion of partial aspects of the same object; you say, for example, that it is one and the same object which you intend under two aspects, and the two aspects, when added together, give an object which is essentially continuous with each aspect in its meaning. And this, I think, constitutes the difference between so-called sense illusion and hallucination: the difference of direction of self completion of the object as first presented. In this sense the assertion of Professor Holt is essentially correct; if it is interpreted as meaning that there is nothing in the immediate presentation of the object to determine its reality or unreality; it is I believe mistaken so far as it means that there is in an absolute sense a given object which is not internally related to its own completion. And the degree to which this claim (as it may be called) is realized without practical falsification of the first presentation is the degree of truth of the first presentation. The stick under water is continuous with the stick out of water, in a way in which an hallucination is not; for the latter can complete itself only backward, i.e., the experience has its relations in the direction of neural process, not in the direction which the image intends. It is by this capacity of indefinite self-completion, and not by any ear-marks, that we judge the reality of a presentation;

but without this capacity, or the claim, we could not have even a presentation.

The reality of an hallucination is not, in the first place, judged merely by vividness or precision. Vividness, in the ordinary sense, is no more a condition of hallucination than is the liveliness of an idea the condition of belief. An hallucination simply cannot be as vivid as a normal waking impression without fulfilling all the conditions of such impression. There is no question of mere brightness of mental image, in the way in which a well made photograph is brighter than a short exposure. For brightness in this sense is a wholly objective matter; when we look at a dim photograph our impression is as precise and clear as when we examine a very sharp photograph. You cannot, that is, define the strength of an hallucination by the supposed objective clearness of a presentation which is really 'there'; you cannot say that the hallucination has all the characteristics of a reality except the third dimension, for example. Such an explanation leaves us wondering why we do not have the hallucination of reality — as well as the 'illusion' — when we contemplate a picture. And it is perhaps in point to offer this one remark on tridimensionality. Three dimensions exist wherever three dimensions are implied. Now in the contemplation of a picture our attitude may I think be analysed into two: we contemplate the reality referred to by the lines and tones, and, we contemplate the lines and tones themselves. A picture is analogous to any of the common figures of optical illusion; the meaning (or reference) of the picture corresponds to the illusory direction of the lines, and the actual arrangements of paint to the 'real' directions. In point of fact the apparent direction of the lines is just as objective as the real direction; the apparent direction is the 'meaning' of the figure. So the tridimensionality of the picture is just as real as the onedimensionality of the surface: so far as it is a picture, so far as it refers to three dimensions, it has three dimensions. An hallucination, also, has three dimensions for the point of view of the hallucinated is the *only* point of view; whereas in the case of a picture there is another point of view which is recognized at the same time. An hallucination is therefore wholly unlike a picture, in that there is one point of view from which it is real, and another from which it does not exist at all; though from the point of view of an outsider it may be what I have previously denominated an intended half-object; i.e., we intend something which from our point of view is wholly inexistent. In order to acknowledge the existence of hallucinations we have partially to concede their truth.*

No comparison with normal experience, according to the considerations above, can give an account of the plausibility of an hallucination, for so far as it exists it has all the features of the real world, and it exists so far as it is believed in. The principle upon which I insist is of course the unity and continuity of feeling and objectivity, the fact that, as dwelt upon in the first chapter, the two are only discriminated aspects in the whole of experience. Take, for instance, a child frightened by a bogey. The child 'thinks it sees' a bear. The meaning of this phrase is by no means self-evident, for we have, I believe, no criterion for saying that the child does or does not see a bear. Such an illusion may be much more, or much less, than a cinematograph bear; Pierre Janet gives examples, from among his hystericals, of the sensation of touch and weight as well. But in a commonplace hallucination (cf. William James in his cabin) the moment of perception is usually I believe very slight indeed, though — and this is an important point — we can never say that it is altogether

* This paragraph is only the detailed examination of a point which falls under the general doctrine here stated: 'Error is without any question a dangerous subject, and the chief difficulty is as follows: We cannot, on the one hand, accept anything between non-existence and reality, while, on the other hand, error obstinately refuses to be either. It persistently attempts to maintain a third position, which appears nowhere to exist, and yet somehow is occupied. In false appearance there is something attributed to the real which does not belong to it. But if the appearance is not real, then it is not false appearance because it is nothing. On the other hand, if it is false, it must therefore be true reality, for it is something which is. And this dilemma at first sight seems insoluble. Or, to put it otherwise, an appearance, which is, must fall somewhere. But error, because it is false, cannot belong to the Absolute; and again, it cannot appertain to the finite subject, because that with all its contents cannot fall outside the Absolute; at least, if it did, it would be nothing. And so error has no home, it has no place in existence; and yet, for all that, it exists. And for this reason it has occasioned much doubt and difficulty.' *Appearance*, pp. 164–5.

absent. In the case of the frightened child, I am not prepared to support the James-Lange theory, but I do not see any priority of image over emotion, or vice versa. There is, if you like, a tendency for emotion to objectify itself,* but the implication is surely mutual, for feeling and image react upon one another inextricably, and the two aspects are so closely related, that you cannot say that the relation is casual.

It is therefore not altogether true or altogether false to say that the child sees a bear. For to take one group of relations of the word 'bear', and say that this group and no other shall constitute the meaning, is not only unwarranted but impossible. The child does not know just what it means when it says 'bear', nor do we know what it means; it does not know just what it has perceived when it has been frightened by a 'bear', nor do we know what it has perceived. For as the difference between real bear and illusory bear is a difference of fullness of relations, and is *not* the sort of difference which subsists between two classes of objects, so the one word must cover both reality and error. The only case in which it is possible in any sense to say that a perception is 'mistaken' is when there is actually before us an object closely enough resembling the object of the erroneous perception to justify our saying that it was this object which we perceived and from which we made false inferences; so that the degree of error which we recognize is in inverse ratio to the degree of similarity between the first and the second perception. The error is thus error because we are able in practice to assume that it was the true object that we perceived the whole time. In practice, that is to say, you can credit the possibility of a false inference from a truly apprehended premiss; but in theory you cannot say that the premiss is truly apprehended in one case and not in the other, for you have no right to say that it is the same premiss. The premiss (here the perception from which we infer) is only *that* premiss with reference to what follows, and in this sense, every inference is a true inference. For in metaphysics there is no concatenation of inferences, but there is a starting-point which expands itself and

* Cf. Lipps, *Vom Fühlen, Wollen, und Denken*, p. 70.

can neither be arrested nor analysed, for the process is not one simply of addition, but of inner development, so that the starting-point itself is altered, and you cannot say absolutely what the starting-point was. When we take these facts into consideration, we find that it is only relatively that we can declare an erroneous object to have been inferred from a true perception. The real object was 'there', and in a practical sense it was that to which the perception referred, but the solution, in which we account for a true and a false perception by summing them up under an identical reference, is essentially a *practical* solution, inasmuch as it involves an *interpretation* of a point of view which we do not accept, that of the error, and an interpretation is essentially unverifiable.

The error is an error then, because we compare it to a cognate reality. It differs from hallucination in that in the latter case there is no cognate reality. The difference is of course of degree only, for we do compare the differences of an identity with respect to hallucination: the room as it really is versus the room plus the spectre, and the fact that it is the same room gives us warrant for affirming error. We only say that an object is unreal with respect to something else which we declare to have been affirmed at the same time and which continues to be real, while the other does not. Now an hallucination has a greater degree of substantiality than an error, because of its greater independence; there is, strictly speaking, nothing to contrast it with except its own unreality. An hallucination, therefore, is not a 'mistake', for it is not attached to the real world in the direction of objectivity; it cannot be interpreted as referring to any object which is actually 'there'. It is attached to the real world, but its real relations are in the direction of physiological foundation, and this involves a much more radical change of point of view than mere error.

We have seen that the hallucination does not differ from the real object by defect of any specific qualities (weight, solidity, internality, etc.) for such a question belongs wholly to another dimension. It does not differ by contrast with some other (real) object which we are said (really) to intend. Reality, we find, is not to be defined by anything in the immediate content.* There is a common form of reconciliation, however, which possesses a high degree of persuasiveness, and which does indeed explain unreal objects of perception in a limited way. The error, the hallucination, and the reality, will all be equally real in themselves, and perhaps ultimately harmonious; but we are in practice concerned only with a very restricted field of reality, a field no more real from the absolute point of view than any of the fragments which we exclude from it. We assume a complex *a-b-c-d*, and we exclude *x-B* fragments of a different alphabet, because we prefer the alphabet of which we have the more letters. The so-called hallucination is real and true when properly understood; when stating an error we really meant a truth. It is only because we have arbitrarily separated one portion of reality from the rest, a separation necessary for experience from finite centres, that we are obliged to relegate the rest to unreality. The world as we are acquainted with it from this limited point of view is an artificial construction, and, our point of view not being large enough to grasp the whole, we consider the rest simply as the debris of our own slight structure. This is perhaps a doctrine of certain idealisms; and it is, so far as I understand, the doctrine of Professor Holt, who says (*op. cit.*, p. 357): 'The . . . content (i.e., an image) simply is, and is in itself neither true nor false.' The idealist asserts, 'We have at first *A*, which possesses the qualities *c* and *b*, inconsistent adjectives which collide; and we go on to produce harmony by making a distinction within this subject. That was not really mere *A*, but either a complex within *A*, or (rather here) a wider whole in which *A* is included. The real subject is *A + D*; and this subject contains the contradiction made harmless by division, since *A* is *c* and *D* is *b*.' (*Appearance*, p. 170).

These two statements seem to me substantially the same. One asserts that the content simply is; the other that the transmuted content is the same content as the first. Both assert, I believe, in

* See Nettleship, *Remains*, I, p. 188, '[T]here is no way of testing the truth or falsehood of an experience except by going beyond it. . . .'

the case of hallucination, that there is a real object present which is interpreted in two different ways, true or false. But we have seen that there is no choice but whether the object be real or non-existent. If the real subject is not A but $A + D$, yet on the other hand the subject to which both c and b referred is A simply, and (for an idealist at least) the quality which refers to a different subject is a different quality; while for Professor Holt there is in illusory experience a real contradiction, and yet (*The New Realism*, p. 366) '. . . by reality we seem to mean the thing most remote from contradiction'.

No account of error in terms of 'dissolution' can ultimately satisfy, though its only justification is its ultimacy (*Appearance*, pp. 170–1). Such an account is ostensibly idealistic, since its criterion is coherence, and ultimate coherence is postulated, so that no purely 'unreal' objects are to be left over, as in a realistic world; but it is compelled to make assumptions of simple correspondence. 'Let us suppose the reality to be $X(a\ b\ c\ d\ e\ f\ g\ . . .)$ and that we are able only to get partial views of this reality.'[40] But in metaphysics it is only by a euphemism that such a partial view is a view of *that* object, rather than a complete view of a different object; and the self-completion of the view involves the affirmation of another reality to which the reality apprehended fails to conform. You may say that the partial view or the hallucination implies its own self-contradiction and transcendence. But in the 'transcendence' of error, I insist, the error, as a real object, is not got rid of. An object is not transcended, though a point of view is; and it is only as we consider the hallucination not as an object, but as an element in a point of view, that it can be said to be 'transcended', 'transmuted', or 'dissolved'. Such a theory as that here outlined by Mr Bradley or by Professor Holt appears unsatisfactory in that the unreality is merely pushed back and not done away with. What we thought was the object was not the object. But we have seen that an object is an object so far as it is thought to be so. The alteration from error to truth is not a change in the object, but a change in the whole situation, and the object, so far as it is an object, must be admitted to persist as a real object in history. The illusion which I have lived through is no more un-real than is Julius Caesar unreal because he is dead. If the world is as essentially connected as idealists would often have us think, the unreal object must still persist and influence reality.*

The situation in regard to hallucinations and in regard to erroneous judgments is not essentially different. The one asserts the existence of an unreal object, and the other the subsistence of an unreal objective; and the line between object and objective, and between existence and subsistence, cannot as we have seen be sharply drawn. Something is asserted to be, which is not; though in order to assert the being of an object we must in some way perceive it. 'The problem of error cannot be solved by an enlarged scheme of relations. . . . For there is a positive sense and a specific character which marks each appearance, and this will still fall outside' (*Appearance*, p. 172). We can thus approach to no solution so long as we regard the world as made up of objects.

We must conclude then that the difference between hallucination and reality is not the difference between an unreal object and a real one. All objects are real, and the unreality is not of them *qua* objects, but because of certain other relations into which (in their reality otherwise than as objects) they fail to enter. An hallucina-tion, we are constantly tempted to forget, is not an object, but a sphere of reality; its existence is internal as well as external. The contradictions which we have to reconcile are not two objects, for objects in themselves cannot contradict each other (this is in agreement, I believe, with Mr Holt) but two points of view, although I should maintain (as against Mr Holt) that the object is inseparable from the point of view.** The hallucination is a whole world of feeling, and the object is simply that world so far as objectified, You cannot, therefore, compare the two objects

---

* Cf. Joachim, *Nature of Truth*, pp. 144–5: 'For precisely that feature in error, which at the time robs it of its sting for the erring person (viz. his untroubled con-fidence in the truth of his judgement), constitutes the distinctive character of error and its power for mischief. And this feature is never annulled and never converted into an element of the fuller knowledge. The triumphant development of astronomy has neither annulled nor absorbed the persecution of Galileo. . . .'

** Though two points of view may intend the same object. See later.

directly, but only through the media of the two points of view of error and truth (though the two viewpoints are in themselves as objective as you please). We are unable to say, however, that one point of view is right and the other wrong, for we thus imply an element of identity, or of identical reference; the assertion of one point of view against another must be made from a third point of view, which somehow contains the first and second. And yet it must be noticed (for I see no way to avoid this hair-splitting) that it is only from the third point of view that the first two are therein contained. For as soon as we have realized that we have reached a third point of view we are already at a fourth, in which the first and second reassert themselves once more. So that it is only so long as we can support a particular point of view (and this involves not recognizing it as such) that we can believe that the contradiction between truth and error is super-seded. To this matter I shall recur later. The chief result that I would emphasize here is that an hallucination involves much more than the assertion of contradictory objects; it involves a change in the subject as well. The *I* who saw the ghost is not the *I* who had the attack of indigestion. In a change of viewpoint, there is some sense at least a total change, and I shall ask in another place just what sort of identity persists.

With imaginary objects we come to a class which is frequently, under the name of assumptions, distinguished sharply from objects of belief, both true and erroneous. I cannot feel that this dis-tinction is needed. On the basis of the previous discussion, it should appear that any object is real in so far as it is attended to, and that when we assert an error or hallucination, we attend not to the object itself but to the experience. When I think of the golden mountain, I think of something which is to that extent real, i.e., what we call its unreality will appear from subsequent relations and not from the immediate presentations. There is, upon this view, nothing which we may call mere presentation. When we speak of presentation, (see my third chapter) we refer to something which was never actually presented, the 'content'; what is presented is really the object, and this is not presented as a presentation, but as real. Undoubtedly it will be objected that we do think of objects as unreal. To this point I shall recur later; here I shall only recall what was said about the object of hallucination; in referring to a past hallucination the direct object is an experience, the indirect object the hallucinatory object. As the imaginary object does not differ essentially from this indirect object, I shall pass to it through a consideration of the object of a past hallucination.

I said that the direct object is an erroneous experience. But this is a real object only to a slight extent, and at the first analysis appears to be an intended object. For it splits into two parts, like other psychological objects: the physiological part and the real part. On the one hand we intend what 'really went on'; if it is certain 'ideas' in the 'mind' then these ideas (Chapter II) dissolve into the physiological process; and nothing 'went on' which cannot be described by the neurologist. On the other hand we intend the object intended by the patient, and this is on our part a true case of assumption as far as it is successful. When we intend an intention, that is to say, we intend something which is real in our world in combination with something which is not real in our world. But the experience as a whole *is* real in our world; other men's experiences are realities with which we come into contact, and which are continually influencing us. Here then, we have cases in which an assumption forms part of a reality: in which an assumption is real not simply as a real assumption (i.e., the fact that we made the assumption is true), but we have to make the assumption in order to apprehend an object which we know to be real. In cases like this we seem to confront a feature of the assumption neglected by Meinong. For the object of the hallucination is not assumed in the way in which objects which we do not know to exist are assumed; the object here is known not to exist. We cannot intend the intention of an object without intending the object itself; this is what I have called the indirect object when the direct object is an experience. And where the experience is an assumption and not an hallucination the matter is still further complicated. Another man 'assumes' the golden mountain;

The Epistemologist's Theory of Knowledge

I intend this experience as an object. I ought theoretically to be able to assume the assumption without committing myself to any attitude toward the golden mountain on my own account; but I find that I am obliged to make an indirect object of the mountain, intend it not only *through* the intention of the assumption, but directly. This immediacy holds true even if the object is something of which I know nothing, and the name of which has no meaning for me. I still *intend* the same object. Here again, in order to apprehend a reality (someone's making an assumption) I am forced to make an assumption myself. According to the account which I have given of psychology, in fact, we make assumptions in the apprehension of a large number of real objects.

I infer from these facts that assumption is not a simple act, but that the term may be made to cover every act from acceptance to rejection; and that the apprehension of an object known to be imaginary does not differ essentially from the apprehension of any other object, unless we have hocus-pocussed an external reality to which ideas are to 'conform'. Can we, in reading a novel, simply assume the characters and the situations? On the contrary, I seem to find that we either accept them as real, (with hallucination as the limiting case) or consider them as *meanings*, as a criticism of reality from the author's point of view. Actually, I think that if we did not vacillate between these two extremes (one of which alone would give the 'photographic' novel and the other the arid 'pièce à thèse') a novel would mean very little to us. The characters and the situations are all 'imaginary', but is there any one act which so apprehends them, cut off and 'floating'? In order to be imaginary, they must be contrasted with something which is real. There must, furthermore, be specific points of resemblance and difference: for the type of reality with which the imaginary object is contrasted must be a type to which the latter pretends to belong. Now so far as merely the imaginary object intends such a reality and falls short, it is not an object of any kind real or imaginary, but falls under what I have said previously of 'mere idea'. If the character in fiction is an imaginary object, it must be by virtue of something more than its being imaginary, i.e. merely

123

intending to be a reality which it is not. It must be, as I said, contrasted with this reality; to be contrasted it must be more than a pure reference; it must have in fact another aspect in which it has a reality of its own distinct from its reference. The fiction is thus more than a fiction: it is a *real* fiction.

We thus analyse the intended object of fiction into its reference and its reality. The reality in its turn is not a simple object but an intended object, for it includes everything from the antecedents of the character in the author's mind, to the symbols which express the character on paper. We may mean the character as a presentation to the author's mind; but a figure in fiction may and often does have an existence for us distinct from what is merely our interpretation of what the author 'had in mind'. Frequently we feel more confidence in our own interpretation of the character than in any account of the genesis and meaning which the author may give himself. This is not always mere accident; no really 'vital' character in fiction is altogether a conscious construction of the author. On the contrary, it may be a sort of parasitic growth upon the author's personality, developing by internal necessity as much as by external addition. So that we come to feel that the point of view from which the author criticizes is not wholly internal to the point of view from which he created the character. Of course this difference should not be insisted upon, for the author may shift from a creative to a critical point of view and back at any moment.* Now a character which is 'lived through', which is real to us not merely by suggesting 'that sort of person' but by its independent cogency, is to the extent of its success real. Treating it as imaginary involves a change of viewpoint. Besides this reality, the character has other relations which are inconsistent with reality. It belongs in other contexts, has relations which are incompatible with its reality. Its unreality, therefore, is not in itself, but in relations extending far beyond itself; its reality is its reference, and its unreality as that to which it refers is its

---

* The combination of criticism and creation is found perhaps in such writers as Molière and Stendhal: whilst the characters of Balzac and Dostoevsky are much more nearly lived through simply.

reality as an 'imaginary' object. And, on the other hand, as an imaginary object it is just as real as anything; it is as a real object that it is imaginary.

An imaginary object has thus two main aspects: its intention to be real and its reality as an intention. As the former it is limited by its paucity of relations; as the latter it exists by virtue of its relations. There is, strictly speaking, no imaginary objective: we attend to a complex which comprehends two points of view — a real object with few relations and an intended object which consists of its relations. When we speak of the character as a fiction we mean a relation between an object real from one point of view and certain entities (ultimately physical) which are real from another point of view. The imaginary object, it will follow, is a highly complex ideal construction. It exists as such only from a third point of view which includes the two just mentioned; but these two also are in the closest dependence upon one another. For the real relations of the intended object (the mental and physical conditions which attended the genesis and realization of that character of fiction) would not be such as they are without the intention to realize a fiction.

At this point I must introduce another complication. The author himself may attend to his fiction not merely as an intended reality (i.e. he may not be and in reality I suppose never is conscious of his fiction from the point of view from which it is real). He may be conscious of the continual *va-et-vient* of ideas in the process of realization; the intended reality shifts and changes as he deserts one outcome for another; and he may be conscious furthermore of the effort to express felt emotions and abstract ideas by 'clothing them in flesh and blood'. So that I do not believe that the author in process of composition is ever, in practice, occupied with a single point of view; or that in practice any moment ever exists when one point of view is in exclusive possession. But the 'imaginary object' has all these relations and in fact *is* these relations.

Finally, I do not see any possibility of saying that the imaginary object either subsists or exists. For when we think of the character in fiction, we go on to think of some aspect in the complex. Becky Sharp exists in the time-order of *Vanity Fair*, but this time-order does not itself exist. Becky exists as an event in the life of Thackeray, and as an event in the life of every reader in the same way that every real person exists as an event in the life of every other real person with whom he comes in contact. But the object denoted by the word Becky does not exist, for it is simply the identical reference of several points of view.

If the evidence which I have offered has any relevance, it should appear that assumption or entertainment is by no means a simple act like acceptance or rejection. The object is not a simple object. There is a simple object which is real in the same way in which an hallucination is real, but this object is only part of the object of the assumption. The chief advantage which this theory pretends to offer over Meinong's is its greater consistency with Bradley's views on floating ideas. The *Annahme*, as I understand it, is such a floating idea. If reality is all of a piece, as the epistemologist believes, then the imaginary must be cut off and floating 'like Mahomet's coffin' between earth and sky. In the theory which I outline, the distinction of objective and subjective, external reality and mental, is unnecessary. Whatever is gathered together in consciousness equally is, and is real or unreal only in relation.

A third class of objects is that of unreal objects. These differ from the two foregoing in that they are neither believed in nor partially believed in, but are intended objects of 'denoting phrases which denote nothing'. In the other two classes there always is an object, although in the case of assumptions the object* dissolves into entities which are not themselves objects but do not fail to exist. We might say that in an assumption the object is real, but is not an object, and that in the intention of an unreal object the object is an object but is not real. The question is, in the words of Mr Russell, whether 'any grammatically correct denoting phrase stands for an *object*'. ('On denoting', *Mind*, 1905, p. 482).

---

* Making a sharp distinction between the object of the assumption and the object of the belief which is one of the points of view entering into the assumption.

The difficulty with Meinong's view, according to Mr Russell, is that such an object may infringe the law of contradiction. The present King of France will both exist and not exist, the round square will be round and not round. The fallacy of this criticism lies, I believe, in treating existence as being for metaphysics as well as for formal logic, a simple predicate.* To say that the present King of France both exists and not exists is no more false than to say that my typewriter both exists and not exists inasmuch as it now exists for me who am looking at it, and not for Mr Russell who is looking at something else. In other words, in asserting existence of any object, we denote existence but do not mean it; and yet, we do mean to denote, and this meaning to denote is an essential part of the denoting.

The difficulty is greatly enhanced by the fact that in the use of any phrase we cannot always be sure to what extent we are meaning the denotation or meaning the meaning, and how far we are denoting the denotation or denoting the meaning. For practical purposes the phrase 'the present King of France' denotes a real object but has no meaning; but this will not do for us, because any denoting phrase which can be used in a proposition means to have meaning, and is therefore not meaningless, and also a phrase cannot denote without likewise having meaning. While we may say, according to Mr Russell, that

(1) 'The present King of France' is a denoting phrase,

we may not say

(2) The present King of France is bald.

It is possible, however, to deny the admissibility of the first of the two propositions, for it implies the partial maintenance of two points of view. I do not see how we can refer to the meaning of a phrase without referring also to its denotation.

Proposition (1) is about 'the present King', but would not be a proposition unless we assumed at one moment the existence of the present King. For if we *know* that 'the present King' denotes

---

* From the point of view taken in this paper, of course, any simple judgment of existence will always be partially false. But this is not precisely the argument used here.

nothing, then it isn't denoting; and if we say that it means to
denote, then we have transported ourselves to a point of view
internal to the meaning, and actually mention the present King
of France. In logic, perhaps, but not in metaphysic, a denoting
phrase may denote nothing. Somehow, obscurely, the object
denoted is acknowledged existence. It is non-existent according
to the practical standards which recognize no degrees between
existence and non-existence; but for metaphysics, it cannot be
denied practical reality without being admitted to some more
attenuated but (if you like) equally real reality.

And notice that the contrast is not at all that between the solid
reality and the idea. This is to confuse denotation with meaning.
'Chimeras do not exist.'*[41] This proposition does not say: Ideal
chimeras do not exist. The chimeras to which existence is denied
are not the chimeras 'in my head' but the real chimeras. But
surely, it will be objected, we do not say: Real chimeras are
unreal! Yet that is in my opinion, just what, from the point of
view of metaphysics, we do say, and any other statement would
be meaningless. The explanation so far as there is one, is simply
this. The phrase, 'real chimeras' can be taken in two ways:
(1) the chimeras which are actually experienced; (2) chimeras
which are 'real'. The word 'real' has in (1) meaning, and in (2)
denotation. On the other hand in order to have meaning in (1),
it must denote something which in experience is actually judged
to be real in sense (2), and in order to have denotation in (2) it
must have meaning in actual experience. By substituting alter-
nately we get

Chimeras such as are experienced, are not real.
Real chimeras (i.e., such as would satisfy all the conditions of
reality) are not experienced — not met with in experience.

Here by denying the predication of denotation of meaning and
vice versa we seem to escape contradiction. But the evasion is only
momentary. For the phrase 'chimeras such as are experienced'
denotes real chimeras, and the phrase 'real chimeras' means

* *Principles of Logic*, p. 115.

chimeras which are actually experienced. Can we say that the non-existent chimeras are real chimeras in denotation and imaginary chimeras in meaning? We have some idea of that to which we deny existence, and the idea, we have seen above, is so far as it is ideal as well the reality which it intends, and we must say similarly of the denoting phrase, that so far as it denotes it denotes a real object.

What has been said of the status of ideas, in a previous chapter, will thus apply to a certain extent to denoting phrases. In each there is the moment of objectivity, so that it implies its own fulfilment in reality, as an object of practical experience. Idea and phrase both denote realities, but the realities which they denote are so far as idea or phrase denotes, identical with the idea or the phrase. It is a mistake, I think, to treat the word as something which barely points to the object, a sign-post which you leave behind on the road. The word 'chimera' or the idea 'chimera' is the beginning of the reality chimera and is absolutely continuous with it, and the 'present King of France' is already partially real. The phrase directs your attention to an object but the object is an object because it is also that object, because the mere hypothetical moment of objectivity is qualified by the characters of the phrase, which are real properties at once of the phrase and of the object. Just as the idea refers to itself, so the denoting phrase denotes itself. But just as an idea is not a thing, and our difficulties arise from trying to treat it as a thing, so a denoting phrase is not a thing. It is not simply *that*, for a mere *that* (which is in fact only a theoretical limit) does not refer to something else; reference is a kind of activity, original or delegated. Like an idea, a word or phrase has existence outside of its objectivity, and a denoting phrase in particular resembles an idea in having an existence which straddles so to speak two moments of objectivity; the one moment being simply those marks or sounds which denote, and the other the object denoted.

This is the only way that I can discover to get over the metaphysical difficulties of unreal objects: to a very large extent we are not dealing with objects at all, and it is only when we try to press an exact meaning that we find language forcing untenable theories upon us. The denoting phrase is not an object, and existence is a complex notion. What we denote when we *denote the denoting phrase is* not the phrase as such, for that is an activity rather than an object, but rather the tendency toward objectification in the direction toward us; that is, the 'word', the written sign, or the *vox et praeterea nihil*. But this object itself is an abstraction and not real, for when you have stripped it of its power, its reference, it is no longer that object, but something quite unrelated to the denoting. It would thus appear that in denoting the object is no more than a moment of objectivity, and that in thinking of a denoting phrase we mean an object which dissolves into two sub-objects and a relation. And this analysis is a falsification, for one object cannot, as we have said, refer to another without being more than an object, and the sub-objects, abstracted from the reference, disappear.

The usefulness of this account will not be at first evident but it may go a little way toward solving the difficulties raised by other explanations. The difficulty of Meinong's theory that there are unreal objects is, as Mr Russell points out, the fact that such objects violate the law of contradiction; and the difficulty of Mr Russell's theory is the contradiction of phrases denoting which yet denote nothing — a pure mystery. The position of Meinong is untenable, I think, only so long as we assume that although objects may exist in various ways, they can exist only in one degree. While it is true that the round square is both square and round, it is not true to say that it is both round and not round, although square may imply, in other contexts, not-round. This is to confuse two planes of reality; so far as the object exists at all it is both square and round, but the squareness and roundness which it has are the squareness and roundness of that degree of reality; the object is not present upon that level of reality upon which square and round are contradictory, though it is none the less, *qua* object, real. Objects exist for us in two ways: As we *intend* an object, the intended object is so far real, and as we experience an object, it realizes itself, and comes to require a certain degree of fullness of relations before it considers itself an object. The ordinary objects (by which we set our standard of reality for the intended objects denoted by the symbols which denote those ordinary or usual objects) are objects of the second sort. But we are accustomed to handle and use them by symbols which merely denote them; we forget that their reality is as much in their meaning as in their denotation, and we take it for granted that they simply are. Nor is this belief error — the matter is much more complicated than that! *As* objects, it is true that they simply are: but unfortunately, in order to be objects, they must be much more; they must be continuous with experience, and continuous with it in a rich and full way. Now commonly we do not treat unreal objects as objects *simpliciter*: the common-sense solution is to treat our 'real' objects *simpliciter*, and our unreal or imaginary objects as more immediately continuous with experience. Yet when we come to *préciser* we find ourselves reversing the proce dure for we discover that it was just this continuity with experience, this fullness of relation, which gave us what we call our real objects, and just the discontinuity, the mere intention, which gave us our unreal objects. The 'unreal' object, *qua* object, is just the bare intention, the object-moment; whereas the 'real' object *is* real because it has so much to draw upon; because if removed it would, we feel, leave so much more of a void in our experience. And yet this unlimited credit is not the object itself; for it is not as such objective. So we are forced to conclude that one object is more real than another — more of an object — by virtue of non-object relations.* Both real object and unreal object are, *qua* objects, equally real; when, both, so to speak, are at the fovea. It is only when we cease to consider either simply as an object, that one appears to be real and the other unreal.

We may say, then, that the unreal object, although it exists, does not violate the law of contradiction.** While it is, broadly speaking, true that the present King of France both exists and

---

* Ultimately, it must be remembered, there are not even relations.

** And I am tempted, by the way, to regard as a dead letter a law which cannot be violated. Is not this law as useless as the vermiform appendix?

does not exist, it is not true in the same sense; for 'exists', as we have seen, is not a simple predicate. I suppose that it will be objected, to this assertion, that any judgment of existence would be rendered a tautology, for it could no more than declare that an object has the sort of existence that it has. Such an objection would in my opinion hold good only if the sorts of existence were cut off from each other like inches along a yard-stick. When we say exists, we mean a degree of existence to be determined by the context, and when we state the subject, we do not need to know the precise degree of reality which it is to have. In other words, a substantive in isolation is not yet even a substantive, for its degree of quality is quite unknown. Which states no more than that a substantive in complete isolation does not exist; for it would be a symbol that symbolized nothing, and hence would not be a symbol at all, but another reality (i.e., certain marks on paper, etc.).

It is essential to the doctrine which I have sketched that the symbol or sign be not arbitrarily amputated from the object which it symbolizes, as for practical purposes, it is isolated (see p. 90). No symbol, I maintain, is ever a mere symbol, but is continuous with that which it symbolizes. Without words, no objects. The object, purely experienced and not denominated, is not yet an object, because it is only a bundle of particular perceptions; in order to be an object it must present identity in difference throughout a span of time. Now of course I do not pretend that there are no objects for the higher animals, or even for the lower; the difference is in one aspect only of degree. But we may say that in any knowledge prior to speech the object is not so much an identity recognized as such as it is a similar way of acting; the identity is rather lived out than known. What we are here concerned with is the explicit recognition of an object as such, and I do not believe that this occurs without the beginnings of speech. We may say if we like that the dog sees the cat and knows it as a cat, though it does not know its name, and I have no objection to this way of speaking loosely. But when we ask in what this knowledge consists, we can only point to a form of behaviour.

The Epistemologist's Theory of Knowledge

Our only way of showing that we are attending to an object* is to show that it and ourself are independent entities, and to do this we must have names. So that the point at which behaviour changes into mental life is essentially indefinite; it is a question of interpretation whether in expression which is repeated at the approach of the same object (as a cat may have a peculiar way of acting at the approach of a dog) is behaviour or language.[42] In either case, I insist, it is continuous with the object; in the first case because we have no object (except from the point of view of the observer, which must not be confused with that of the patient under examination), and in the second case because it is language which gives us objects rather than mere 'passions'. Or at least we have no objects without language.

I know that it will be objected that I am here confusing the genetic with the structural standpoint; and in reply I can only urge, that I have found the two organically related, and that I cannot admit that metaphysics may analyse and find truth in one part of the analysis, discarding the other. The object, you will say, is now known as independent of the word, though like enough without words we might not have come to know objects. It is true, I reply, that when we mean an object with a word we mean the object and not the word, and we might mean the same object by a different word, though I think that you quite under-estimate the closeness with which particular words are woven into our reality. But the object which we denote in this sense is the object *qua* object, and not the bundle of experiences which the object means. The object *qua* object would not exist without this bundle of experiences, but the bundle would not be a bundle unless it were held together by the moment of objectivity which is realized in the name. I am very far from meaning that it is the act of naming which makes the object, for the activity does not proceed from one side more than from another. Objects cannot arise without names, and names never spring up without objects, ready to be

---

* This is not to say that the *phenomena* of attention are not observable among animals, but that such phenomena need not be in every aspect interpreted as those of *attention*.

133

applied to the first objects to which they seem appropriate. Nor do I mean that the object did not exist until it was known, but only that it has not the character of objectivity until it is known as an object.

The name is not the object, certainly. We may say more truly that it is a category through which one grasps the object (if anyone has a taste for categories), but even this will not state the case correctly, if the category is conceived as something subjective, contrasted with the object. I should prefer to speak of the name as the moment of denotation; it is not that which is denoted, obviously, or merely a convenient means for denoting something which exists in complete independence of the name. It denotes an object which is not itself, and yet, when we ask just what this object is which is denoted, we have nothing to point to but the name. We do not denote any qualities of the object, as such; we do not, that is, denote any definition which could be given of the object; we denote not its *whatness* but its *thatness*. And we must not forget that even 'that' is a name; if I ask you to what you refer, you may simply point to the object and say 'that'; you mean, if you like, a certain bundle of perceptions, but unless what you mean has this name 'that' it is not an object. The simplest thing that a thing can be is to be 'that', is to be merely object; and we are not denoting 'that', and it is not object, until we have these two words at our disposal. Try to think of what anything would be if you refrained from naming it altogether, and it will dissolve into sensations which are not objects; and it will not be that particular object which it is, until you have found the right name for it.

This relationship of thing and name has interesting aspects on the other side. If we cannot say that we have that object until we have that name, since each name is a different way of organizing a set of experiences, so on the other hand we have not really got that name until we have the right object. It is evident that a name is not a name unless it is the name of something, that the feeling of a meaning, if ever so faint, will just make the difference between a name and a mere *Laut-complex*. Now just as an object which we

134

cannot name is as yet only the adumbration of that object, so the name of which the object is not as yet distinct is only the adumbration of that name; we sometimes find ourselves guilty of using very specific names when for all that we know the name is equivalent merely to 'object'. Yet the name implies particularity. As we may fancy, if we like, objects wandering about waiting to be met with and be named (like the animals in the Garden of Eden), so we may fancy names wandering about in our heads waiting for objects. But such is an hypothetical limit which is never reached. Now as imaginary objects and imaginary spheres of reality are not 'in our heads', any more than the 'real' world is, names may be names of real objects in imaginary spheres. The 'present King of France' is not the name for anything in the 'real' world — but in the real world the 'present King of France' is not a name at all: supposing that there were such a real world cut off from all imaginary worlds, 'the present King of France' would be a mere noise — in the real world.

This, however is a digression. Though we cannot say that we have either name or object (to recur to the beginning of the last paragraph) until we have the complete object for that name or the complete name for that object, yet the point at which this mystic marriage occurs is not exactly determinable. This should make a little clearer my observations on the child's imaginary bear (p. 115). The child means 'bear', we may say, without really knowing what bear means; yet so far as it has reacted to the bogey in the same way as it would to a real bear, the name 'bear' in the child's mind has a real bear to back it up. The name has terminated in an experience, and as even the word 'chimera' terminates in an experience in so far as the word is admitted to have a meaning, and not merely itself to *be*, the word has a real object.

The discussion of real and unreal objects will proceed with eternal fruitlessness so long as we maintain the belief that there is one consistent world of the real and that the rest is illusory. Nor do we advance a step farther by affirming that everything is real, for this alteration merely crams all the unreality into thought which was formerly in perception, and in nowise resolves the question. The whole difficulty, I believe, arises from taking existence as a simple concept. Whereas, I have tried to show, we can never extricate the denotation of 'real' from its meaning. The process of development of a real world, as we are apt to forget in our theories, works in two directions; we have not first a real world to which we add our imaginings, nor have we a real world out of which we select *our* 'real' world, but the real and the unreal develop side by side. If we think of the world not as ready made — the world, that is, of meaning for us — but as constructed, or constructing itself, (for I am careful not to talk of the creative activity of mind, a phrase meaningless in metaphysics) at every moment, and never more than an approximate construction, a construction essentially practical in its nature: then the difficulties of real and unreal disappear. Theories of knowledge usually assume that there is one consistent real world, in which everything is real and equally real, and that it is our business to find it. They do this largely, I suppose, because common sense does the same thing, not realizing that the denotations of real and unreal may hold good for a practical point of view and not for a metaphysical. While the real world of epistemology is hard and fast, its *whatness* and its *thatness* inseparably geminated, the real world of practice is essentially vague, unprecise, swarming with what are, from a metaphysical point of view, insoluble contradictions. We forget that what has grown up from a purely practical attitude cannot be explained by a purely theoretical. The real and the unreal are, from the outside point of view which we attempt to take as epistemologists, equally real, and our consequent troubles are due to the fact that these contrasts arose and have their meaning, only from the internal point of view which we have abandoned in seeking an explanation.

We can never, I mean, wholly explain the practical world from a theoretical point of view, because this world is what it is by reason of the practical point of view and the world which we try to explain is a world spread out upon a table — simply *there*! The plight into which we put ourselves is however inevitable, for the theoretical point of view is the inevitable outgrowth of the practical. We arrive at objects, as I have tried to show, by meaning objects; sensations organize themselves around a (logical) point of attention and the world of feeling is transmogrified into a world of self and object. We thus have an object which is constituted by the denoting, though what we denote has an existence as an object only because it is also not an object, for *qua* object it is merely the denoting, the projection of shadow of the intention; as *real* object it is not object, but a whole of experiences which cluster round the point of denotation.* Now in practice do we use the complex meaning or only the denotation? I do not see any final answer to this question. For a theoretical account of the practical attitude would be a description from an outside point of view; and a 'practical' account would give merely the theory of our practice. A theory of practice or a practice of theory would be equally beside the mark: the first inevitably would reduce everything to meaning and the second would reduce everything to denoting. So far as objects are objects, we always intend to denote them, of course; but in practice, they are only objects partially or occasionally, and we cannot decide to what extent.

Practice, and this is the difficulty (though all our difficulties are perhaps one in different forms) is shot through with theory, and theory with practice. The hypothetical transition from sensation to subject-object, which I have attempted to outline, is a speculative activity. The assumption of a real world is a theory; nothing, in fact, is merely found. And the distinction between theory and practice can nowhere be positively drawn; whether we are setting up an assumption 'for our own ends' or purely from the love of speculation, is everywhere matter for a relative distinction. In general we may say, nevertheless, that the sharper and more complete the lines, the more theoretical the account; and in this way, when we attempt to define practice we get a theory, and a theory may incorporate itself into our practice. Hence our theory will be found full of practical motives and

---

* Not always, or even usually, a 'bundle of sensations'. All the associations and ideal relations are here meant.

practical consequences, and our practice will be found to be largely based upon speculation.

To return, after this long digression, to our objects, I conclude that we can never give an exact description or explanation of the relations of the real and the unreal. For we have no difficulty with the matter at all until we begin to think (yet this thinking was forced upon us originally by the practical difficulties of illusion). Practically, as I said before, we use 'real' in two senses, and thus skip, within the practical, between practical and theoretical points of view. 'Chimeras do not exist.' A theoretical account of this might be, I said, 'real chimeras are not real.' This might be the theoretical account of what we really say, or the theory which we practise, or the theoretical account of the theory that we practise. Or we might give either of the alternatives which I offered earlier. But in every judgment there arises the contrast between reality and unreality.* A contrast which from a point of view (outside the sphere of interest of that judgment) is unjustified in the form in which it presents itself, and always means something different. But in the end these accounts are simply interpretations which have greater or less utility. 'Chimeras do not exist.' If we understand this it needs no explanation, if not we can find none. 'The King of France is bald.' This is true or false or meaningless according to its context and bearing. That the theory needs working out in great detail I cannot see. It would be tying knots in the east wind. We have secured, I think, a general principle, and have seen why it neither demands nor admits complete elaboration.

What I have been saying may seem to have no direct bearing upon the metaphysics of Mr Bradley, but the whole position taken here throughout the discussion of the epistemological attitude has been in support of this metaphysic. For from this point of view the problem of knowledge does not exist; the distinction between inner and outer, which makes the epistemologist's capital, cannot stand. We have seen that the word 'idea' does not

---

* So that we may not too perversely say that judgment is the predication of an ideal content of Unreality.

refer to something ('thing') which intervenes between the object and the percipient, but is a stage in the process of realization of a world. The object so far as there is an object is presented to the knower without mediation of category or other psychological apparatus. Knowledge, that is to say, cannot be defined in terms of anything else; and so far as there is any problem, it has its origin in the fact that knowing is not simply knowing, but has another aspect. And why this is, I have to some extent attempted to show. We tend to think of objects — of things — as being objects under any and every condition: if they are not objects when they are not known, then the only alternative, we think, is that they disappear altogether. But we have seen that even within experience objects could not be objects unless they were much more; and their objectivity, their being denoted, is only a moment of their reality; a moment which we say metaphorically is supported by an act of the will, although I should never admit that the situation was due to the subject side any more than to the object side, or that the notion of activity was ultimately possible in any sense.

The real world, if the real world means the world of real objects, is thus something with which we are in immediate contact, and indeed quite real — as real as you like — though varying and unprecise. Its 'relation' to the knower is however not here in question, inasmuch as knowledge is not a relation. The real world is not inside or outside; it is not presented in consciousness or to consciousness as a particular grouping of entities, for as presented it is not in or to consciousness at all: it simply is. There is no meaning, I think, in saying that in knowing consciousness is either active or passive, or that there is an 'awareness' beyond the mere psycho-physiological phenomena of attention; or that consciousness 'is' its object or is different from its object. But knowing, we have found, is only part of a larger process of experience, and the point at which we have real knowing is never precisely determinable. There is always, in our experience, a real world 'external' in a restricted sense, for there is always, in any existence worthy of us, a real object of attention, and so far as there is, the object

139

is directly known but not directly experienced; for the object, to be an object, is always meant to be something more than its abstracted qualities, and to be directly known cannot be directly experienced.* But the object as object cannot be self-supporting. Its objectivity is merely externality, and nothing in reality can be merely external, but must possess being 'for' itself. Yet to mean it as an object means to mean it as more than an object, as something *ultimately* real. And in this way every object leads us far beyond itself to an ultimate reality: this is the justification for our metaphysics.

The objects which are apprehended by every finite centre are as apprehended real. The question arises, how the worlds of these various centres may be said to form one world; inasmuch as there is no 'objective' criterion for reality in the sense of an external solid world to which our individual presentations should conform. The real world, I have insisted, consists in the common meaning and 'identical reference' of various finite centres. This leads to a question, cardinal in the philosophy of Mr Bradley; the question of finite centres and solipsism.

* 'Sugar is obviously not mere whiteness, mere hardness, and mere sweetness; for its reality lies somehow in its unity. But if, on the other hand, we inquire what there can be in the thing beside its several qualities, we are baffled once more. We can discover no real unity existing outside these qualities, or, again, existing within them.' *Appearance*, p. 16.

CHAPTER VI

Solipsism

It should be evident why the conclusions already reached demand an examination of Solipsism; but I will briefly recount them. We have seen that there is no other object than that which appears, and its appearance as an object gives it, in an absolute sense, all that objectively it could possibly mean. If you are willing to make the abstraction of a world appearing to one finite centre alone, then we may say that nothing in this world is false or erroneous, but is what it is and as it is. And outside of the objectivity of objects appearing to finite centres, there is no objectivity at all, for we have found that objectivity and thinghood are aspects under which reality appears; true but partial aspects; and that the reality of a 'thing' (we are here painfully hampered by language) is in no wise limited to its thinghood. But beyond the objective worlds of a number of finite centres, each having its own objects, there is no objective world. Thus we confront the question: how do we yoke our divers worlds to draw together? how can we issue from the circle described about each point of view? and since I can know no point of view but my own, how can I know that there are other points of view, or admitting their existence, how can I take any account of them?*

Solipsism has been one of the dramatic properties of most philosophical entertainers. Yet we cannot discard it without recognizing that it rests upon a truth. '[T]hough my experience is not the whole world, yet that world appears in my experience, and, so far as it exists there, it *is* my state of mind. . . . And so, in the

* The controversy between Brunetière and France is rather instructive, showing a muddling of the question by two men who are not philosophers, but have each his own personal solution in practice.

141

end, to know the Universe, we must fall back upon our personal experience and sensation'.[43] This doctrine I should like to develop in something of detail, with regard to real objects. And in doing this I must summon in the theory of points of view upon which I have relied before. Obviously, by the conclusions at which I have arrived, it is true to say that the real world is real because and in so far as it appears to a finite centre, and yet it has in each appearance to mean to be more — to be real, that is, only so far as it is not an appearance to a finite centre. From a point of view completely detached, reality would contain nothing but finite centres and their several presentations; but from the point of view of each centre, there is an objective world upon which several points of view are trained, and to which they all refer. And it is just the confusion of these two truths which gives the stuffed solipsism of the philosophers. I have tried to show that there can be no truth or error without a presentation and discrimination of two points of view; that the external world is a construction by the selection and combination of various presentations to various viewpoints: and that the selection which makes reality is in turn made possible by the belief in reality: unless we assumed the existence of a world of truth we could not explain the genesis of error, and unless we had presentations of error as well as of truth we could not make that construction which is the real world. But taking the various experience-centres as real, we may inquire, with reference to this manifold, in what consists the reality of the one world which they all suppose.

Every finite centre, we may lay down, intends an 'objective' world; and the genesis of this intention is an obscure and difficult matter. We cannot say anything on the subject which will be more than an interpretation; but I offer this as a provisional account, admitting that any account that expresses itself as a temporal sequence can be only very provisional indeed. The first objects, we may say, with which we come into contact are half-objects,* they are other finite centres, not attended to directly as objects,

---

* But of course they are not apprehended as such. There is a felt conflict and difference between centres, and this breaks up the unity of our expression.

but are interpretations of recognized resistances and felt divergences. We come to interpret our own experience as the attention to a world of objects, as we feel obscurely an identity between the experiences of other centres and our own. And it is this identity which gradually shapes itself into the external world. There are two (or more) worlds each continuous with a self, and yet running in the other direction — *somehow* — into an identity. Thus in adjusting our behaviour to that of others and in co-operating with them we come to intend an identical world.

We ask then naturally, in what the identity consists, beyond the 'identical reference'. Yet while the question is natural, I cannot admit that it is legitimate. And I should like to recall various passages in which I have spoken of 'identical reference', especially in connection with memory. It appeared there that an element of identity might be present, without our being able to isolate it as an actuality. The relation found to obtain between an experience and our recollection of it was not a relation of mere resemblance, but involved a common reference to a third reality, which was known simply as *the* reality which both intended. A reference to an identity, it was laid down, *is* the identity, in the sense in which a word *is* that which it denotes. An identity is intended, and it could not have been intended, we say, unless it was there; but its being 'there' consists simply in the intention, and has no other meaning. What do we mean when we say that two people see 'the same' object? We think loosely that the identity consists in the fact that when one looks at the object from the same angle as the other, the two images before the two minds are the same. We compare two prints of the same negative and find them identical. But there is evidently a difference between the two cases (a difference which is ultimately, however, one of degree) in that the difference between the two points of view is a difference, if we choose to consider it so, of two whole worlds; the identity is of two realities which cannot possibly be set side by side and compared. All identity is ideal ... 'in this sense that it involves the self-transcendence of that which is identical' (*Appearance*, p. 526). And this fact, that identity in the

content of two minds is an identity of ideal meaning may cause us
to ask if even in the simplest case of comparison the identity is
not equally ideal. All identities which two objects may present,
though simply of colour or of form, involve a self-transcendence
on the part of the particulars. This means, of course, only that we
have no knowledge of mere particulars. But it means also that the
identity between one man's world and another's does not consist,
as we readily are lead to believe, in one world which is the world
of right perception, and which is, apart from being known, exactly
what it is when we know it.

This fact, furthermore, ought to be self-evident. Identity, we
have learned, is nowhere bare identity, but must be identity in
diversity. If we are hit on the head with the same club, the club is
only 'the same' because it has appeared in two different contexts.
There are two different experiences, and the sameness is quite
ideal. We do, of course, partially put ourselves at the point of
view of the man who hit us, and partially at each other's points
of view; and it is the interweaving of these viewpoints which gives
us the objective club. There is no one club, no one world, without
a diversity of points of view for it to be one to. The 'real' turns out
everywhere to be ideal — but is none the less real for that. Point to
anything as 'independent' of a finite centre, and you find that what is
independent is merely the moment of objectivity — and this is ideal.

When I say that there is one world because one world is intended, I have still stated only half of the case; for any explanation in terms of 'because' (a term made necessary by the weakness
of human conceiving) can be only misleading unless we turn it
about the other way as well. Let us say, therefore, that we are
able to intend one world because our points of view are essentially
akin.* For it is not as if the isolated individuals had contributed
each a share and entered into partnership to provide a public

* '... the foundation of it all is this, that no phase in a particular consciousness
is merely a phase of the apparent subject, but it is always and essentially a member
of a further whole of experience, which passes through and unites the states of
many consciousnesses, but is not exhausted in any, nor in all of them, as states,
taken together. It is true that my state of mind is mine, and yours is yours; but
not only do I experience in mine what you experience in yours — that would be
consistent with the total independence of the two minds — but I experience it

world. The selves, on the contrary, find themselves from the start in common dependence upon one indifferent Nature. Nature assumes, inevitably, a different aspect to each point of view; no two finite centres, we may say, apprehend the same Nature, yet each centre has pressed upon it the fact that from the one Nature it with all its neighbours sprang. To claim that this is inconsistent with the isolation of our monads is to confuse the genetic and the structural standpoints. My mind, that is, I must treat as both absolute and derived; absolute, in that it is a point of view from which I cannot possibly escape (to which indeed I am bound so closely that the word escape is without meaning); derived, in that I am able, by virtue of the continuity of mind with the non-mental, to trace in some way its origin, with that of other minds, from an indifferent material. Biologically, we see minds in a common medium, and treating minds thus as objects, we conclude their content to be similar just as we find their physical structure and their environment similar. And from this point of view we talk about the one 'external' world and the various 'mental contents' referring to it. For minds may be intended objects; and their objectivity is continuous with their subjectivity, the mental continuous with the merely mechanistic. But we must remember that no view is original or ultimate: when we inquire into the real world, however, we mean the world from the viewpoints of finite centres as subjects only; we mean the real world for us now, not from the point of view of some further developed mind tracing its ancestors and the world they lived in.

The world, we may insist, is neither one nor many except as that one or many has meaning in experience, and it is either one or many according as we contemplate it altogether as an object, talking still, if you will, of minds, but meaning rather the phenomena which mind presents to an observer: or as we treat the world as finite centres and their experiences. From the first point of view the world is *a priori* one; from the second point of view

differently from you, in such a way that there is a systematic relation between the two contents experienced, and neither is intelligible or complete without the other.' Bosanquet, *Prin. of Ind. and Value*, p. 315.

the world is *a priori* many; and I am convinced that this is the
only form in which monism or pluralism can appear. And the two
views are so far from antagonistic as to be complementary. The
self, we find, seems to depend upon a world which in turn depends
upon it; and nowhere, I repeat, can we find anything original or
ultimate. And the self depends as well upon other selves; it is not
given as a direct experience, but is an interpretation of experience
by interaction with other selves (see *Appearance*, p. 219). The self
is a construction, and yet the[44]

The doctrine of finite centres appears in an interesting light
when compared with the theories of Leibniz, with which it has
very striking affinities. Compare, for example, the celebrated
paragraph of the *Monadology*, 57: 'And as the same town, looked
at from various sides, appears quite different and becomes as it
were numerous in aspects; even so, as a result of the infinite
number of simple substances, it is as if there were so many different
universes, which, nevertheless, are nothing but aspects (*per-
spectives*) of a single universe, according to the special point of
view of each monad.' (Latta's ed., p. 248).

It is easy to raise objections to Leibniz's form of statement,
but I think that his aim becomes more intelligible in the light of
our 'finite centres'. Leibniz appears to have made the error, it is
true, of identifying a point of view with a felt unit, or self.* And
for Leibniz the internal view of the world was ultimate. But the
assertion that 'the monads have no windows' in no wise entangles
him in solipsism, for it means (or may be taken to mean) what Mr
Bradley means in saying that our knowledge of other finite centres
is only through physical appearance within our own world. When
an event occurs within my world it occurs to me, but I would not
be I apart from the event; it is from the beginning coloured by my
personality, as my personality is coloured by it. A theory of
internal relations is thus implicit; and perhaps a recognition of
the continuity of terms and relations contributed to the doctrine

---

* 'Finite centres of feeling, while they last, are (so far as we know) not directly
pervious to one another. But ... a self is not the same as such a centre of experience.' *Appearance*, p. 464.

of monads. If anything could appear as really acting upon and altering the self, the latter would take the place merely of one object among others, and so far as it is subject, we can conceive it as having aspects, but not relations. And when we qualify our world by the recognition of another's it is not his world as it is in reality, but his world as it affects us that enters into our world. We arrive at the belief in other finite selves in a sense by inference, though on the other hand it is assumed that these other selves exist, or they could not be phenomenally represented in our world. To say that I can know only my own states, accordingly, is in no wise the foundation of solipsism, unless it were possible that I should know my states as my states, and as nothing else, which would be a palpable contradiction. What I know is my own state simply as the real aspect (knowledge as object) seems to take precedence of the ideal aspect (knowledge as meaning). The statement that 'monads have no windows', therefore, means only that the objectivity of one's world is ideal; and that the reality is experience.

And the pre-established harmony is unnecessary if we recognize that the monads are not wholly distinct, and that the subjective self is continuous with the self as object. A monad was for Leibniz, I believe, something real in the way in which a physical organism is real: he imagined the monads, that is, on this analogy, and identified the monad with the phenomenal soul. Now for Bradley the finite centre, (or what I call the point of view), is not identical with the soul. We may think provisionally of finite centres as the units of soul life; units, however, whose limits cannot be drawn with any precision. For we vary by passing from one point of view to another or as I have tried to suggest, by occupying more than one point of view at the same time, an attitude which gives us our assumptions, our half-objects, our figments of imagination; we vary by self-transcendence. The point of view (or finite centre) has for its object one consistent world, and accordingly no finite centre can be self-sufficient, for the life of a soul does not consist in the contemplation of one consistent world but in the painful task of unifying (to a greater or less extent) jarring and incompatible ones, and passing, when possible, from two or more discordant viewpoints to a higher which shall somehow include and transmute them. The soul is so far from being a monad that we have not only to interpret other souls to ourself but to interpret ourself to ourself. Wherever a point of view may be distinguished, I say, there a point of view is. And whereas we may change our point of view, it is better not to say that the point of view has changed. For if there is a noticeable change, you have no identity of which to predicate the change. The point of view, we may say, is as such purely ideal; it can hardly be said to possess existence.

The doctrine here set forth must not however be construed as a psychical atomism, or anything of that sort; the finite centres (as I understand the matter) are not all of one size or shape, but vary with the context. Thus, while one soul may experience within itself many finite centres, the soul itself may be considered in a loose sense as a finite centre. The more of a personality it is, the more harmonious and self-contained, the more definitely it is said to possess a 'point of view', a point of view toward the social world. Wherever, in short, there is a unity of consciousness, this unity may be spoken of as a finite centre. Yet neither the term 'soul' nor the term 'self' is ever identical with the term 'finite centre'. 'Then from immediate experience' (at any level) 'the self emerges, and is set apart by a distinction' (p. 464).[45] To realize that a point of view is a point of view is already to have transcended it: what was merely a picture in two dimensions (if you please) becomes a real landscape with an infinity of aspects as the 'what' disengages itself from the 'that'. The 'what' continues to be recognized as a true qualification of the 'that', but is as well a qualification of the apprehending consciousness, and the real object results from the abstraction and comparison of the various points of view.

What constitutes the difference, therefore, between two points of view, is the difference which each is capable of making to the other. There could be no such thing, we may say, as a single finite centre, for every experience implies the existence of something independent of the experience, something capable, therefore, of being experienced differently, and the recognition of this fact is already the transition to another point of view. Treating the experience as the reality, we may say (*ibid.*, p. 464) that 'Finite centres of feeling, while they last, are . . . not directly pervious to one another'. So far as experiences go, we may be said in a sense to live each in a different world. But 'world' in this sense, is not the world with which solipsism is concerned; each centre of experience is unique, but is unique only with reference to a common meaning. Two points of view, in consequence, can be said to differ only so far as they intend the same object, though the object, we have seen, is only such with reference to a point of view.

Two points of view take cognizance of each other, I suppose, by each making a half-object of the other. Strictly speaking, a point of view taking note of another is no longer the same, but a third, centre of feeling; yet it is something different from a centre of feeling: more properly a self, a 'construction based on, and itself transcending, immediate experience'.[46] Everywhere, we must constantly remind ourselves, the difference is one of degree; and when one finite centre affects another merely as an alteration in its experience, and is not consciously recognized as another centre, we can hardly say that there is a self. And inasmuch as the finite centre is an experience, while the self is one aspect in that experience, and again contains and harmonizes several experiences, we may say that the self is both less and more than such a centre, and is ideal. For this reason it is more correct to say that a self passes from one point of view to another, than to say that one point of view takes cognizance of another. But a finite centre may be made an intended object by a self, and thus enter into another finite centre, though not as such. Thus we may continue to say that finite centres are impervious. Identity we find to be everywhere ideal, while finite centres are real. When we ask what, finally, in the finite centre is the common property of several finite centres, intending the same object, the answer is: nothing — 'really', everything — 'ideally', and in practice there may be a greater or less amount of community. We may schematize it crudely thus:

Solipsism

In Theory
- Really
  - *a* — All unique, but
  - *b* — All may be an intended object in another finite centre.
- Ideally
  - *c* — The intended object in each centre is public. Whatever is made an object is public.

In Practice
- Really
  - *d* — Two finite centres may be judged from a third point of view to resemble each other.
- Ideally
  - *e* — As much is public as is not discernably different.

Note that in (*d*) the resemblance is predicated on the ground of behaviour; it is predicated not of the centres as such, but inferred from ideal identity of object when we observe two organisms behaving in the same way toward what from our point of view is the same object for each. Similarly we may infer the resemblance of a centre of feeling in another self to one of our own, though the two experiences as such have no relation to each other, not even the relation of difference.

The reflection of the world in finite centres, of a world which is real only as it appears in those centres, is a form of monadism which, as we find, by no means implies a 'pluralistic universe'. These centres are not things, and to speak of them as 'independent' or 'isolated' is more misleading than illuminating. When we speak of such isolated centres we mean always souls. A centre of experience, however, is always 'below, or else wider than and above, the distinction' (*Appearance*, p. 468) of self and not-self. A soul, or a self (though the two terms are not everywhere equivalent (see *ibid.*, p. 464, note)) is always the 'creature of an intellectual construction';[47] it is never simply given, but depends upon a transcendence of immediacy. And a doctrine of solipsism would have to show that myself and my states were immediately given, and other selves inferred. But just because what is given is not my self but my world, the question is meaningless. The process of the genesis

150

of the self and of other selves is ultimately perhaps unknowable, since there is no 'because' which we can assign. There are reasons for believing that externality was recognized as force or as spirit before it was apprehended in the form of objects; as the primitive life, furthermore, is immersed in practice and incapable of the degree of speculative interest necessary for the constitution of an object. On the other hand we may say that we know other finite centres only through the mediation of objects. 'The immediate experiences of finite beings cannot, as such, come together. . . . A direct connexion between souls we cannot say is impossible, but on the other hand, we find no good reason for supposing it to exist. . . . We may assume then that souls do not influence each other except through their bodies.' (*Appearance*, pp. 303–4).

The issue here hangs only on the exact meaning which we are to attribute to the word 'knowledge'. We become acquainted with the existence of other souls, we may say, through the influence which they exert upon the content of our experience, but we only become acquainted with that content as content through the postulation of foreign activities influencing it, so that we are lead to distinguish a 'what' and a 'that'. But the question at what point either becomes explicit is essentially unanswerable. We can only say that the self, the other selves, and the objects do in this process become more precise, and clear. And we can say that we have no knowledge of other souls except through their bodies, because it is only thus that we can enter into their world.

On the other hand, as we need to be reminded, we have no direct (immediate) knowledge of anything: the 'immediately given' is the bag of gold at the end of the rainbow. Knowledge is invariably a matter of degree: you cannot put your finger upon even the simplest datum and say 'this we know'. In the growth and construction of the world we live in, there is no one stage, and no one aspect, which you can take as the foundation. Radical empiricists assume that we have an 'immediate' knowledge of a mysterious flux, and criticists assume that we know sense-data, or universals, immediately, as we do not know objects or other selves. But where we are first interested in knowing, there is the first thing known; and in this way we may say (if we choose to employ this language) that that of which we have immediate knowledge is the external world, for without externality there is no knowledge. The platform of knowing, in fact, is the assertion of something to be known, something independent of me so far as that knowing is concerned. No absolute assertion about the object's dependence or independence is made or implied. Hence if the object is only my state both object and I must be strangely transmuted, for I only know myself in contrast to a world. And it will be equally true to say that I am only a state of my objects. But, it will be objected, if knowledge of objects belongs to a world which is admittedly a construction, should not we return to the primitive experience to find reality? Or are you not tacitly affirming that the world in which we find ourselves now is the real world, and is the process of which you speak not a process in knowledge rather than a process in reality? This question introduces us to the relation of thought and reality, and the doctrine of degrees of truth, with which I intend to close.

CHAPTER VII

Conclusion

The task of this concluding chapter is merely to weave together the conclusions of the other chapters and present them if possible as a coherent whole; and to touch as well upon certain consequences which have not as yet appeared. We may draw, I believe, certain inferences as to the nature of reality which will forbid us to accept either an idealistic or a realistic philosophy at its full value. But I believe that all of the conclusions that I have reached are in substantial agreement with *Appearance and Reality*, though I have been compelled to reject certain theories, logical and psychological, which appear in the *Principles* and elsewhere. Out of absolute idealism we retain what I consider its most important doctrines, Degrees of Truth and Reality and the Internality of Relations; we reject the reliance upon 'consciousness' or 'the work of the mind' as a principle of explanation. With regard to objects, I have reached the conclusion that all objects are non-mental; and with regard to mental activity, I conclude that we find only physiological activity or logical activity, both independent of, and more fundamental than what we call the activity of mind. But the materialism, which (as exemplified particularly in the work of Mr Bosanquet) from one point of view may very justly be said to lie at the basis of idealism, presents only one aspect of the situation. If the aim of my examination of structural psychology was to demonstrate that the more accurately and scientifically one pursues the traces of mentality in the 'mind' of the individual, the less one finds; so on the other hand my examination of the epistemologist's world has been an attempt to prove that the more closely one scrutinizes the 'external world', and the more eagerly and positively one plucks at it, the less there is to see and touch. Cut off a 'mental' and a 'physical' world, dissect and classify the phenomena of each: the mental resolves into a curious and intricate mechanism, and the physical reveals itself as a mental construct. If you will find the mechanical anywhere, you will find it in the workings of mind; and to inspect living mind, you must look nowhere but in the world outside. Such is the general doctrine to which my theory of objects points.

There are other conclusions bound up with this doctrine. As to the problem of knowledge, we have found that it does not exist. Knowledge, that is to say, is not a relation, and cannot be explained by any analysis. We do not say, however, that in knowing the 'mind' comes into immediate and direct contact with the object, for we find that such an assertion has no great meaning, for there is no 'mind' for the object to be brought into contact with, and with the physical organism the object known may or may not be in direct contact. And to say that the object is dependent on or independent of the knower — this again I think is a statement of no great importance, though of the two alternatives I think that it is perhaps truer to say that the object is independent. For *qua* known, the object is simply there, and has no relation to the knower whatever, and the knower, *qua* knower, is not a part of the world which he knows: he does not exist.

This bare and hypothetical knowledge, I admit, is only a part of what serves our use. We do not, in point of fact, simply know: we make tentative and hardly formulated theories of knowledge in practice, theories which go to make up our real knowledge. And again there is much in that which we call knowledge which is not knowing in what narrowly speaking is the only legitimate sense. It is these two disturbing factors which complicate and indeed create the problem. The point is worthy of great elaboration, and even in so sketchy a discussion as the present may occupy us for several moments. What I mean is this. Theoretically, that which we know is merely spread out before us for pure contemplation, and the subject, the I, or the self, is no more consciously present than is the inter-cellular action. But I do not say that such a condition is or was ever realized in practice; indeed, such knowledge would hardly be of any profit. The real situation is rather that we have as I have tried to show in the first chapter a felt whole in which there are moments of knowledge: the objects are constantly shifting, and new transpositions of objectivity and feeling constantly developing. We perceive an object, we will say, and then perceive it in a special relation to our body. In our practical relations with objects we find it convenient and even essential to consider the object's relation to ourself as itself an object; in many cases this is what is important. This self may be primarily the body, but the body is in felt continuity with the spiritual self. And in cases where the presence of the self is an important part in the meaning of the knowledge, a sort of theory of knowledge is at work. It is this sort of knowing, I presume, that induces us to think of knowing as a relation. There is a relation between the object and the self: a relation which is theoretical and not merely actual, in the sense that the self as a term capable of relation with other terms is a construction. And this self which is objectified and related is continuous and felt to be continuous with the self which is subject and not an element in that which is known. As it is metaphysics which has produced the self so it is epistemology, we may say, which has produced knowledge. It is perhaps epistemology (though I offer this only as a suggestion, and to make clearer the sort of thing that I mean) that has given us the fine arts; for what was at first expression and behaviour may have developed under the complications of self-conscious-ness, as we became aware of ourselves as reacting aesthetically to the object.

In any case, we are constantly developing and rectifying our perceptions by comparison with other perceptions; we are con-stantly on the lookout for error, and our recognition and allow-ances for error already nominate us as epistemologists; for this means that we have a tentative working theory of our relation to the external world. It is thus, to a certain extent, a theory of knowledge that gives us an external world, but a theory which cannot hold beyond a certain range of practice. Theory and practice are, we find, inextricable: for without theory we should not have our present practice, and without the practice in which it finds its application the theory would be meaningless.

No theory of knowledge, consequently, can establish itself on a firm foundation by defining the sort of relation that knowing is, for knowing is not a relation; in order to give any account of knowing we must bring in the terms which are related, and these terms are only provisionally definable. We can only define the thing as known and the knower as knowing, and yet both things and knower imply a transcendence of these limitations, a transcendence which has no end. And it is only so far as our knowledge is invalid or incomplete that research into the nature of knowing can bear any fruit, for when we believe our knowledge to be correct and sufficient we can do no more than describe the physical relations between our body and the object apprehended. In any analysis of knowledge, knowing is assumed; we can to a certain extent explain false knowing in terms of true knowing, but we cannot explain true knowing in terms of anything else.

While we cannot, it thus appears, 'know knowing', what we can do is to describe in a general way the process of transition and development which takes place when there is an organism which is a part of the world and yet is capable to a certain degree of contemplating the world. Knowing, we have said, is inextricably intertwined with processes which are not knowing; knowing, furthermore, is only an aspect in a continuous reality. We can to a certain extent describe the rise and decay of objects. And this is not because the object is essentially dependent upon consciousness, for I do not know what such a phrase would mean: but because consciousness and its object are both only evanescent aspects in reality. When we think what knowing really means in our experience,[48] how essentially relative its meaning is, for it can never escape from the ultimate limits of its own meaning; and even when it consciously intends to be unconditionally true, that unconditionality is within these bounds and no statement can claim to be true except when it has meaning. So that while we make no attempt to explain knowledge, we can I think offer a limited insight into its nature by indicating the fringe through which it passes into something else, and by indicating the stages of the process which we call degrees of truth.

My first step, in accordance with this plan, was to attempt to suggest the reality out of which subject and object are sorted, and upon which as background they have their meaning. Our first step is to discover what experience is not, and why it is essentially indefinable. We saw that within experience there presented themselves the two aspects of ideality and reality, but that this distinction did not correpond to a division among objects: for a thing is real or ideal only in relation. We found that what we call the 'real' in experience is largely ideal, and that what we call 'ideal' is largely real, and that Reality itself would not be reality without its appearances. The ideal and the real, the mental and the non-mental, the active and the passive, these are terms which apply only to *appearance*; which take their meaning from narrow and practical contexts.

In seeking for the object of knowledge, then, we need no investigation into the process of knowing or the nature of an external world. It is not true that we deny the existence of an external world, for anyone who pursues this path of inquiry will come to the conclusion that this question is ultimately meaningless. But demanding at the start what it is that we know for most certain (and this method deserves the name of empiricism as much as anything does) we find that we are certain of everything, — relatively, and of nothing, — positively, and that no knowledge will survive analysis. The virtue of metaphysical analysis is in showing the destructibility of everything, since analysis gives us something equally real, and for some purposes more real, than that which is analysed. In analysing knowledge, we merely educe the fact that knowledge is composed of ingredients which are themselves neither known nor cognitive, but which melt into the whole which we call experience.* The analysis of the object, from this point of view, reveals the fact that in asking what the object

---

* 'For while the This cannot be brought into the unity of knowledge, it is unquestionably a part of reality. And so the failure of knowledge to bring it into unity with itself involves that the part of the object which *is* brought into unity with the subject is only an abstraction from the full object. . . . The result is that we know objects, so to speak, from the outside. . . .' McTaggart, *Heg. Dialectic*, p. 222.

is we merely turn in a circle. The object is not its qualities, for these are simply enjoyed with respect to the object; the object as such, it transpires, is merely the point of *attention*; that which an electron, a Balkan league, my table, whiteness, have in common as objects is just the *moment of objectivity*. The objecthood of an object, it appears, is the fact that we intend it as an object: it is the attending that makes the object, and yet we may say with equal truth that if there were no object we could not attend. The fact that an object is an object, in this light, appears to be the least fact about it, and its reality is due to the experiences which cluster around it: an object is real, we may say, in proportion to its relations outside of its objectivity.

I should be asked, no doubt, whether an object ceases to be an object on ceasing to be known. This question I feel justified in refusing to answer, since I cannot feel that anyone who understands what I have meant by objectivity will ask it. For practical purposes, undoubtedly, we may think of objects as objects when they are not objects to anyone, or I may think of an object as an object when it is the object of your attention and not of mine: but in general to think of an object is (not to *think* of it as my object, but) to make an object of it. The object, I mean to say, is none the less *real* when I am not attending to it, but it is no longer object. For all that 'object' means is a connection of certain experiences with a moment of objectivity, of experiences which would not exist as what they are unless connected in *that* way with *that* point of attention (moment of objectivity), and of a point of attention which would not be without those qualities, for those qualities essentially refer to it, and *it* is only the fact of their intended reference. The object is a complex of experiences with a reference, and the reference itself is an experience. But we cannot say that it is *my* experience, for I am only I in relation to objects. The object thus resolves itself into experience. But this by no means implies that the object does not persist outside of my experience, or that another subject may not know the same object. For in making this last statement we have so shifted the stage properties that 'object' no longer means exactly the same thing.

Conclusion

This should have been made clear by the discussion of solipsism. Wherever I intend an object, there an object is; wherever two people intend the same object, there an identical object is; and wherever we together intend the existence of an object outside of our knowledge, there an object does exist outside of our knowledge; but we must not forget that in all three of these cases we have theory as well as practice. From one point of view we know that the object exists; but from another point of view this is mere hypothesis: we have a certain latitude, that is, as to what we shall take for granted, and we may put ourselves at the individual or the social point of view, as we please; but we must not forget that unless we make allowance at the start for the equality of their claims to validity we shall be left with a most uncomfortable hiatus, for we can never deduce the one from the other.

It is difficult to tell when we are assigning to a word only such precision and *portée* as is justified in practice, and when we are going beyond use into pure speculation which will make no difference to our practice. We may easily be overawed by language, and attribute to it more philosophic prestige than it really deserves. The word 'object' means a certain type of experience and the theories involved in that experience: theories which lose their meaning beyond a certain point. The only way in which we can handle reality intellectually is to turn it into objects, and the justification of this operation is that the world we live in has been built in this way. At the same time we are forced to admit that the construction is not always completely successful. While we can to a certain extent treat relations as if they were terms, we find with such entities as ideas that to treat them so is almost a step backward rather than a step forward, inasmuch as we can only apprehend their reality by putting ourselves in the place of an obscure world and abandoning a clear and scientific one. There is left psycho-physics and rational psychology. There have developed, I mean to say, certain objects which I have denominated half-objects, having much of the character of objects without being wholly apprehensible. Their nature is that they do not belong to any point of view, but depend for their existence

Conclusion

upon our apprehending two points of view at once, and pursuing neither. Thus the 'mental' would have no place in a 'real' world such as the scientist intends, and the real world would consist in the relations of points whose entire existence was relation: whose reality consisted in their external relations. And it is obvious that such a view is in its way quite as tenable as any other: a theory which reduces reality to mathematical relations of simples is continuous with our ordinary tendency toward objectification, and hence is not less 'true' in the usual sense, than any other; inasmuch as objectification is the creation of a new world, and the assertion that the two worlds are the same is an act of faith, only to be contrasted with another act of faith to the effect that the two are not the same.

The fundamental difficulty is this. When we attend to an object we do not know precisely what it is that we denote or that we mean. In any case of ocular error this fact is patent, and is more than suggested by the discussions of the *Theaetetus*. When I mistake one object for another, I can say loosely that the real object was the object which I 'really' saw, and upon the sight of which I made a mistaken inference. But you never can tell at precisely what point the mistake occurred; how much that is to say was received unaltered from without and how much was constructed from within. We have come upon this *impasse* in theorizing upon bears: far as the object is experienced as *that* object so far it *is* that object, and the rectification is a matter of further experience, through which the illusory object and the real object are bound together in an (ideal) identity of meaning in a practical world. It is, in fact, this real world, which is not metaphysically the real world, that unites the false and the true in a common reference, and thus makes the false false and the true true. Now there is precisely the same difficulty when we explain an appearance by a reality: when we appear only to be revealing the reality of the appearance we may be said to be only presenting another appearance, and the greater the dissimilarity that we find between the two the more certainly our constructio: falls apart into two worlds.

Conclusion

The object of attention, in the first place, has not certain definite limits: its 'that' and its 'what' exhibit a degree of looseness in practice. The object can be the same object though its description more or less vary, and the same description can preserve itself through an indefinite variation of the attention. We never can say, actually, to exactly what we are attending; it is never the hypothetical point and it is to a large extent the ideal synthesis of data by meaning which constitutes the point of attention. I look at a bottle, and the point to which I attend is the bottle; though not necessarily the real bottle, for there may be perhaps no real bottle there; so that we may say the real point of attention is the intended object. In this sense, attention is the intention to attend. The attention is not in practice attention to a point, but to a *that* which is a *that* because it has a single meaning. A *that* which we did not qualify as a *what* would not be even a mere *that*. On the other hand the two aspects of the real object, the *thatness* and the *whatness*, are always distinct because of their difference in meaning; so that we say, in different senses, that we attend to the object which is *that* and *what*, and that we attend literally to the *that* alone. Inasmuch as the *that* is the point of reference of its common qualities, its persistence depends upon our recognition of the community of meaning of the qualities, and this community of meaning is ultimately practical. It is ultimately in every case a question of practice how far any group of qualities constitutes one object, and metaphysics depends upon our ability and good-will to grasp appearance and reality as one. And this limitation is as true of one sort of metaphysic as of another.

Regarding the matter from this light, we must to a certain extent put our theories to the pragmatic test. An account of reality, or of any field of it, which has the appearance of going to the point of substituting a new type of objects for the old will be a true theory and not merely a new world, if it is capable of making an actual practical difference in our attitude toward the old, or toward some already accepted object, so that there may be an identity uniting differences of quality. It is obvious that it is this

161

felt identity between appearance and reality that will constitute explanation, and that the identity is a fragile and insecure thing. Adhering to a strictly common-sense view (which may be defined, I presume, as that which insists on the reality of the more primary objects) the theories of speculative physics seem perhaps as chimerical and uncalled-for as those of metaphysics. There is however considerable difference. A science is such because it is able to deal with objects which are all of one type; and the aim of each science is to reduce reality (so far as reality comes within the purview of that science) to one type of object, and the ultimate type of object I should suppose (acknowledging my incompetence to speak) to be points in mathematical relation. But physical theories (so far as I can pretend to be informed, from popular accounts), are apt to end in mystery, inasmuch as the final object is often not an object at all; if the ultimate is some kind of energy or motion it is not an object but at most a half-object, since it possesses some internality. At this point a theory would become metaphysical, passing from one type of object to another; and two types can only be held together by an act of faith.

It is not within my present purpose or capacity to schematize the various types of object and their relations. Chapters II and III were devoted to one of the most important classes, that of the half-objects of psychology. Chapter IV endeavoured to set forth the ideality of all objects, and the relativity of the distinction between 'real' objects and 'ideal' objects; finally,[49] with the difference between real and unreal objects, and the analysis of imaginary objects and assumptions. The fifth chapter was engaged upon the object as the object of one and as the object of several knowers; the resolution, on the one hand, of the object into experience, and its maintenance as identical reference. We have thus distinguished broadly several types; things, half-objects, double objects, and objects of reference. Half-objects are such as exist, like ideas, only from an internal-external point of view; double objects are such as exist as objects from two points of view, like mental images, hallucinations and objects in fiction, which have a reality in their own space and time, and a different

Conclusion

reality in our space and time.* Objects of reference are such as unreal objects, where the reality of the object consists in barely more than the object's being intended (and perhaps 'sensations' and categories, which are supposed to be enjoyed and not contemplated, belong in this class: for the being of such objects consists in their not being objects). All these types, and 'universals' and 'particulars' as well, may be reduced, in a certain aspect, to things;** for things are the lowest order, so to speak; and on the other hand the thing is analysable into intended objects (qualities) and the intention (or moment of objectivity). But every transformation of type involves a leap which science cannot take, and which metaphysics must take. It involves an *interpretation*, a transmigration from one world to another, and such a pilgrimage involves an act of faith.

In a transformation of object-type there is a change of point of view; in a metaphysical theory there is an attempt to bind together all points of view in one.

And this, I think, should show us why the notion of truth, literal truth, has so little direct application to philosophic theory. A philosophy can and must be worked out with the greatest rigour and discipline in the details, but can ultimately be founded on nothing but faith: and this is the reason, I suspect, why the novelties in philosophy are only in elaboration, and never in fundamentals. There are two uses of the word truth, as we are apt to forget in philosophizing: the truth or error of the metaphysician does not concern the historian in any literal sense. The historian sets out in search of truth from a different gate. And of course the only real truth is the whole truth. I have called attention to the real world (Chapter V), as the felt background against which we project our theories, and with reference to which our speculations have their use. We all recognize the world as the same 'that'; it is when we attempt to describe it that our worlds fall apart, for as we have seen, the same 'that' can only persist through a limited range of whatness. But just as we all admit the

* This depends, of course, upon the continuity of symbol and symbolized.
** These can of course be double half-objects as well.

world to be the same world, though we cannot specify in precisely
what respects, for there are no precise respects, so we feel that
there are truths valid for this world, though we do not know what
these truths are; and it is with this sort that the refined and
subtilized common sense which is Critical Taste occupies itself.
The true critic is a scrupulous avoider of formulae; he refrains
from statements which pretend to be literally true; he finds fact
nowhere and approximation always. His truths are truths of
experience rather than of calculation.

Even these lived truths are partial and fragmentary, for the
finest tact after all can give us only an interpretation, and every
interpretation, along perhaps with some utterly contradictory
interpretation, has to be taken up and reinterpreted by every
thinking mind and by every civilization. This is the significance
of the late Samuel Butler's epigram to the effect that the whole
duty of man was to serve both God and Mammon: for both God
and Mammon are interpretations of the world and have to be
reinterpreted. It is this sort of interpretation (which formally
consists I believe in transformations of object-type) that the
historian, the literary critic, and the metaphysician are engaged
with. Yet the difference between interpretation and description
remains probably a question of degree. When the objects dealt
with are close enough to the physical foundations of our existence
to be in practice identical for all individuals, so that only one
point of view is involved, we get truths which are equally true for
everyone; and to what extent differences of opinion are tenable,
and how deep into the body of a science these differences may
sink, are questions which each science must work out for itself. . . .
And if you wish to say that only those truths which can be
demonstrated can be called true, I will acquiesce, for I am as good
a materialist* as anybody; but though materialist, I would point
out what a little way such truths bring us. For materialism itself
is only an interpretation, and we cannot assert that all the types

* 'For how instructive and how amusing to observe in each case the conflict of
sensation with imported and foreign experience. Perhaps no truth after all could
be half so rich and half so true as the result of this wild discord — to one who sees
from the centre.' *Appearance*, p. 172.

of object which we meet are reducible to this one type of thing.
Any assertion about the *world*, or any *ultimate* statement about
any *object in* the world, will inevitably be an interpretation. It is a
valuation and an assignment of meaning. The things of which we
are collectively certain, we may say our common formulae, are
certainly not true. What makes a real world is difference of
opinion.* I remember a phrase of Eucken's, a phrase which had a
certain *entrain* about it: *es gibt keine Privatwahrheiten* (there are
no private truths). I do not recall the context, and am not concerned with the meaning which the phrase had there; but I should
reverse the decision, and say: All significant truths are private
truths. As they become public they cease to become truths; they
become facts, or at best, part of the public character; or at worst,
catchwords.

If these reflections are meant to be taken seriously, I shall be
told, what excuse is there for a philosophy of the absolute? a
philosophy which transforms objects to the drastic extent of
transforming them all into one, and then declaring that this is no
object at all? Such a question, though natural, would show I
think a complete ignorance of the nature of the 'dialectic process'.
The fact that we can think only in terms of things does not
compel us to the conclusion that reality consists of things. We
have found from the first that the thing is thoroughly relative,
that it exists only in a context of experience, of experience with
which it is continuous. From first to last reality is experience, but
experience would not (so far as we know) be possible without
attention and the moment of objectivity. We are able to distinguish a growth in clearness of the object, a detachment and
independence which it seems to have in greater degree in relation
to the higher forms of life: so that we can say, from our point of
view, that subject and object emerge from a state of feeling. We
can I think say this truly from our point of view. At the same time
we must remember that in saying anything about types of
consciousness different from our own, we are making statements

* The materialism advocated is in substance, I think, the materialism of Mr
Bosanquet.

about worlds which are different from ours, though continuous. Truth on our level is a different thing from truth for the jellyfish, and there must certainly be analogies for truth and error in jellyfish life. So that what in one aspect is a development of the real world is from another aspect a new world. And yet the statement that there is such a development will be true so far as it goes.

And we have the right to say that the world is a construction. Not to say that it is *my* construction, for in that way 'I' am as much 'my' construction as the world is; but to use the word as best we can without implying any active agent: the world is a construction out of finite centres. Any particular datum can be certain only with regard to what is built upon it, not in itself: and every experience contains the principle of its own self-transcendence. Every experience is a paradox in that it means to be absolute, and yet is relative; in that it somehow always goes beyond itself and yet never escapes itself. The simple error of mistaking one man for another illustrates this well enough. There is an ideal identity which persists between experiences and rectifies our judgments; and it is this identity, together with the transcendence, which gives us degrees of truth. This theory simply asserts that a reality, a *that*, may persist under different conditions of *whatness*, though the *that* be indefinable, i.e. though we do not know what *that* it is that has persisted. We never know, in any assertion, just what, or how much, we are asserting.* We denote a *that* which as like as not turns out not to be the *that* that we thought it was; it continues to be the same *that* but with very different qualities: and the truth in question is found by continually analysing the given and widening its relations. Knowledge means a greater control over the material, and this control can only be given by increasing and developing the content. Whether we say that this is a new world or not is a matter of practical convenience. But we do *intend* it to be the same, and we feel that it is the reality which we failed at first to

* 'No judgement is ever entirely severed from a larger background of meaning, though the background may be relatively obscure except at that portion of itself which is thrown into relief and formulated as *this* judgment.' Joachim, *Nature of Truth*, p. 113.

grasp. The cruder and vaguer, or more limited, is somehow contained and explained in the wider and more precise, and this feeling of identity is all that is needed for the postulation of identity.* No judgment is limited to the matter in hand: you affirm that something is something else; and in the simple analytic judgment of sense you posit a 'that' to deny it. The judgment which you make is true only within the range of your experience; for it is the use you make of it that determines its meaning. And furthermore no judgment is true until you understand it; and you never wholly understand it, because 'understanding' experience means merely knowing how to use it; so that what we actually know of a judgment is not its truth but its utility (and truth never *is* utility). That at which we aim is the real as such; and the real as such is not an object.

Thus the process toward the theoretical goal returns upon itself. We aim at a real thing: but everything is real as experience, and as thing everything is ideal. When we define an experience, we substitute the definition for the experience, and then experience the definition; though the original experience may have been itself a definition: but the experiencing is quite another thing from the defining. You start, or pretend to start, from experience — from any experience — and build your theory. You begin with truths which everyone will accept, perhaps, and you find connections which no one else has discovered. In the process, reality has changed, in one sense; for the world of your theory is certainly a very different world from the world from which you began. To the builder of the system, the identity binding together the appearance and the reality is evident; to anyone outside of the system it is not evident. To the builder the process is the process of reality, for thought and reality are one; to a critic, the process is perhaps only the process of the builder's thought. From the critic's standpoint the metaphysician's world may be real only as the child's bogey is real. The one thinks of reality in terms of his

* 'The sciences of botany, of the physiology of the senses, of the physical conditions of colour, &c. — these may be said to absorb and to preserve the "truth" of such judgements as "this tree is green".' *Ibid.*, pp. 112–13.

system; the other thinks of the system in terms of the indefinite social reality. There occurs, in short, just what is sure to occur in a world in which subject and predicate are not one. Metaphysical systems are condemned to go up like a rocket and come down like a stick. The question can always be asked of the closest-woven theory: is this the reality of *my* world of appearance? and if I do not recognize the identity, then it is not. It will not do to say that my denial reasserts, unless I see that it does. For a metaphysics to be accepted, good-will is essential. Two men must *intend* the same object, and *both* men must admit that the object intended is the same.

We are forced to the assumption that truth is one, and to the assumption that reality is one. But dissension rises when we ask the question: what one? Our system has pretended to be about the world of those who do not accept it as much as about the world of those who do. And the world, as we have seen, exists only as it is found in the experiences of finite centres, experiences so mad and strange that they will be boiled away before you boil them down to one homogeneous mass. Thus calamity menaces our theory whether it be a theory of coherence or of correspondence. If of correspondence, where can you say that there exists the world to correspond? For such a world would be susceptible to all the criticisms which we have directed against the objects within the world. And if of coherence, it serves us no better; for what is it that coheres? ideas, we shall be told, and not realities; and the whole structure is a faquir's show for a penny.

In part, I believe, these objections are trivial and in part mistaken. The notion of correspondence, as applied here, exhibits merely a case of the seduction of psychology. There is no question of correspondence (I have tried to show), there is no mere 'idea', except ideally in practice, when we find an 'objective' world because we have other people's 'ideas' which clash and conflict with our own. How can the notion of correspondence apply in metaphysics until we have a social metaphysical background as we have a social background for our non-metaphysical theories? And this will never be. So long as our descriptions and explanations can vary so greatly and yet make so little practical difference, how can we say that our theories have that intended identical reference which is the objective criterion for truth and error? And on the other hand our theories make all the difference in the world, because the truth has to be *my* truth before it can be true at all. This is because an 'objective' truth is a relative truth: all that we care about is how it works; it makes no difference whether a thing really is green or blue, so long as everyone behaves toward it on the belief that it is green or blue. But a metaphysical doctrine pretends to be '*true*' simply, and none of our pragmatic tests will apply. The notion of correspondence will not do, for it has no meaning here. The notion of consistency fails in the same way, if it is not merely 'ideas' that we are examining, but reality. The Absolute, we find, does not fall within any of the classes of objects: it is neither real nor unreal nor imaginary. But I do not think that supersubtle defence is necessary. A metaphysic may be accepted or rejected without our assuming that from the practical point of view it is either true or false. The point is that the world of practical verification has no definite frontiers, and that it is the business of philosophy to keep the frontiers open. If I have insisted on the practical (pragmatic?) in the constitution and meaning of objects, it is because the practical is a practical metaphysic. And this emphasis upon practice — upon the relativity and the instrumentality of knowledge — is what impels us toward the Absolute.[50]

Notes

Many of Mr Eliot's references are given in an abbreviated form which the reader can easily expand by consulting the *Selected Bibliography*. Minor inaccuracies in Mr Eliot's references and within his quotations have generally been corrected wherever they occur in the 1916 texts. It is only in those cases where a reference is called for but is either not given at all, or else given in a confusing or significantly different form, that an additional note has been provided here. Within the texts, these end notes are designated by raised numbers whereas Mr Eliot's own footnotes are designated by asterisks.

Anne C. Bolgan

Knowledge and Experience in the Philosophy of F. H. Bradley:

CHAPTER I

page   16. 1. Bradley, *Essays on Truth and Reality*, 161.
page   25. 2. Bradley, *Essays on Truth and Reality*, 170.
page   28. 3. Bradley, *Appearance and Reality*, 407.
page   28. 4. Bradley, *Appearance and Reality*, 407.

CHAPTER II

page   41. 5. The three quotations here are from Moore, 'The Nature of Judgment', 177.
page   43. 6. Bosanquet, *The Essentials of Logic*, 75.
pages 47–8. 7. Mr Eliot's quotations from pages 3 and 4 of Bradley's *The Principles of Logic* are slightly inaccurate and some connecting sentences which clarify the idea considerably have been omitted. The passage, with the relevant parts added, reads as follows:

'For logical purposes ideas are symbols, and they are

nothing but symbols. And, at the risk of commonplace, before I go on, I must try to say what a symbol
is.

'In all that is we can distinguish two sides, (i) existence and (ii) content. In other words we perceive both
that it is and *what* it is. But in anything that is a
symbol we have also a third side, its signification, or
that which it means. . . .

'But there is a class of facts which possess an other
and additional third side. They have a meaning; and
by a sign we understand any sort of fact which is
used with a meaning. The meaning may be part of the
original content, or it may have been discovered and
even added by a further extension. Still this makes no
difference. Take anything which can stand for anything else, and you have a sign. Beside its own private
existence and content it has this third aspect. . . . A
sign is any fact that has a meaning, and meaning
consists of a part of the content (original or acquired),
cut off, fixed by the mind, and considered apart from
the existence of the sign.'

page **52**. 8. In the original typescript, this sentence reads: 'You
cannot say simply " is identical with a", but you say
" is identical with a, with regard to the identity of B
with b" and vice versa.' The sense, however, clearly
requires the insertion of the capital letter A in the
spaces left open and they have therefore been added to
the 1916 text.

page 55. 9. This sentence makes sense if we alter the final
phrase to read: '. . . but about the present future.'

page 55. 10. The phrase is Bradley's. See *Essays on Truth and
Reality*, 40.

pages 55–6. 11. Mr Eliot's meaning here is easily clarified if we
read the passage as follows:
'The defect, in that it was vaguer, less of an idea, than
the world of others; the superiority, in that the shadows

pointed toward a reality, which, if it had been realized, would have been in some respects a higher type of reality than that of the ordinary world. Compared to it, the ordinary world would be less real, and that which the ordinary world might be said to "mean".'

page 62. 12. Stout, *A Manual of Psychology*, 60.

page 66. 13. The first sentence quoted from Alexander in this paragraph is from page 6 of 'Mental Activity in Willing and in Idea', whereas the remaining three quotations are from pages 7, 13, and 1 respectively of 'On Sensations and Images'. The first of these three quotations should begin with the sentence, 'I stated roundly that mind consisted of conations . . .', and the second, according to the original, should read as follows: 'The imaging of an external or physical thing is of course mental. What is here maintained is that the image itself is non-mental, or external, or I am prepared to say physical.'

page 67. 14. The sense here requires the deletion of the word 'is' and the insertion of the word 'involves'. The sentence would then read: 'Sensation as known always involves some degree of crude perception.'

page 68. 15. This reference, as are all those to *Con. Psych.*, is to Alexander, 'Foundations and Sketch-plan of a Conational Psychology.'

page 70. 16. The reference is to a passage from page 3 of Alexander, 'The Method of Metaphysics and the Categories' wherein he says: 'I propose to say that the mind is enjoyed and its objects contemplated.'

page 76. 17. All three of these articles have been reprinted in Bradley's *Collected Essays*, volume II. For the reader's convenience, therefore, Mr Eliot's references have been transposed to this more generally used and easily accessible volume.

page 76. 18. *Collected Essays* II, 366.

page 77. 19. *Collected Essays* II, 375.

page 77. 20. *Collected Essays* II, 368.

page 77. 21. *Collected Essays* II, 369.

page 77. 22. *Collected Essays* II, 370.

page 79. 23. The sense here requires the omission of the entire
third line, and of the first word in the fourth line as
well. The sentence would then read:
'For internally, their relations among themselves are
determined only by the real world from the point of
view of the subject, and externally by the real world
from somebody else's point of view. . . .'

page 79. 24. *Collected Essays* II, 368.

page 80. 25. *Collected Essays* II, 382.

page 80. 26. *Collected Essays* II, 385.

page 80. 27. *Collected Essays* II, 484.

page 80. 28. *Collected Essays* II, 520.

page 80. 29. *Collected Essays* II, 497.

page 82. 30. These sentences are not to be found in the article
cited but, in this same article, Bradley does make a
statement closely similar to the one quoted. It reads:
'There is in attention never more than one object, the
several "objects" being diverse aspects of or features
within this.' *Collected Essays* II, 431.

Chapter IV

page 94. 31. The sense here requires the insertion of the word
'not'. The sentence would then read:
'The distinction, consequently, between *Ausdruck* and
Bedeutung must not be drawn too closely.'

page 94. 32. Russell, 'Meinong's Theory of Complexes and
Assumptions (III),' 515.

page 95. 33. Mr Eliot's meaning here is easily clarified if we
alter the passage to read:
'Now it may be asked whether a relation to its terms is
apprehended as an object in the same way as is the
object, and whether in any complex there are not two
superiora—the relation uniting, and the whole complex.'

page 97. 34. Russell, 'Meinong's Theory of Complexes and Assumptions (I),' 207.

page 97. 35. Meinong, *Uber die Erfahrungsgrundlagen unseres Wissens*, 99–100.

page 99. 36. Russell, 'Meinong's Theory of Complexes and Assumptions (II),' 352.

page 103. 37. The reference is to Peirce, *Collected Papers* Volume II, Book II, Chapter 3, 'The Icon, Index, and Symbol,' 156–73.

page 104. 38. Mr Eliot's meaning here is easily clarified if we alter the passage to read:

'It consequently transpires that neither the word alone is the object (for there is no word alone), nor the logical meaning (which is an abstraction and cannot be grasped without the word), nor the total of word and meaning (for there is no total — word and meaning being continuous, and the continuity not an object).'

page 107. 39. The passage quoted is from pages 7–8 of Russell's 'On the Relations of Universals and Particulars' but is quoted in a slightly inaccurate way. It should read as follows:

'If, on the other hand, we consider what may be called "real" space, *i.e.* the inferred space containing the "real" objects which we suppose to be the cause of our perceptions, then we no longer know what is the nature of the qualities, if any, which exist in this "real" space, and it is natural to replace the bundle of qualities by a collection of pieces of matter having whatever characteristics the science of the moment may prescribe.'

page 119. 40. Bradley, *Appearance and Reality*, 170.

page 128. 41. The passage referred to in Bradley's *The Principles of Logic*, 115 reads as follows:

'Let us take such a denial as "Chimaeras are non-existent". "Chimaera" is here ostensibly the subject, but is really the predicate.'

page 133. 42. The sense requires the insertion of the word

'there' between 'dog' and 'is'. The sentence would then read:

'[I]t is a question of interpretation whether in expression which is repeated at the approach of the same object (as a cat may have a peculiar way of acting at the approach of a dog), there is behaviour or language.'

CHAPTER VI

page 142. 43. Bradley, *Appearance and Reality*, 229.

page 146. 44. Page 186 of the original typescript ends with this dangling phrase. Page 187 then follows immediately with the new paragraph beginning 'The doctrine of finite centres . . . ,' and continues exactly as given here on page 146. Some material, intervening between these two paragraphs, has obviously been removed. The only other difficulty of this same nature arises at the end of the very last page of the presently existing typescript where, again, the page ends with an incompleted sentence. In both cases, the argument being formulated is identical with that which Mr Eliot goes on to develop in his *Monist* articles — more especially the second one entitled 'Leibniz' Monads and Bradley's Finite Centres.'

page 148. 45. Bradley, *Appearance and Reality*, 464.

page 149. 46. Bradley, *Appearance and Reality*, 465.

page 150. 47. Bradley, *Appearance and Reality*, 468.

CHAPTER VII

page 156. 48. The sense here requires the insertion of the words 'we find'. The passage would then read:

'When we think what knowing really means in our experience, we find how essentially relative its meaning is, for it can never escape from the ultimate limits of its own meaning. . . .'

page 162. 49. The sense here requires the insertion of the words 'it dealt'. The passage would then read:

Notes

'[F]inally, it dealt with the difference between real and unreal objects, and with the analysis of imaginary objects and assumptions.'

page 169. 50. The unfinished sentence 'For if all objectivity and all knowledge is relative' with which the last page of original typescript ends has been omitted here. See Mr Eliot's *Preface* and Note 44.

The Development of
Leibniz' Monadism*

The study of *Monadology* may be comprised in three stages. In the first we isolate the work; with no other aid than the philosophical counters which itself employs, we attempt to draw its fantastic world around us and find it real. Perhaps we supplement it by searching in other works of Leibniz for elucidations of points which are not clear; but in any case we take the *Monadology* as a creed and test our possibilities of belief. No philosophy can be understood without this preliminary effort to accept it on its own terms; but its true value can never be extracted solely in that way. The perfected or the summarized form of any system is the starting point, not the terminus of study. We must effect a radical restatement, find in it motives and problems which are ours, giving it the dignity of a place in the history of science when we withdraw from it the sanctity of a religion. In losing the consistency of a closed system, it gains the consistency of reason, is attached to something larger than itself. Russell and Couturat have accomplished this revaluation for Leibniz. But beside the leading motive, the reason of a philosophy, there are other strata both below and above: prejudices, traditions, suggestions, motives which imperfectly assimilate to the central motive, all of which combine to give to the system the form which it has. The present essay is merely a preface to the investigation of these forces.

There are influences of suggestion, influences of tradition, personal influences, and, moreover, there is more than one conscious

---

* Reprinted from *The Monist* XXVI (October 1916) 534–56. Translations have been added for this edition.

interest. Among influences of the first sort upon Leibniz (none of them of the highest importance) I should class a variety of authors whose contributions to Leibniz are more verbal than profound. Leibniz' reading was wide beyond any point of selection, and he appears to have derived some entertainment from such philosophers as Giordano Bruno, Maimonides, and the Averrhoists.* Bruno is a classic example of influence in the most superficial sense. It is not certain, nor is it important, at what period Leibniz became acquainted with Bruno's works. For the probability that Leibniz was struck by the figurative language, that Bruno may have been in the background when Leibniz wrote some of his more imaginative passages, there is evidence enough. For the probability that Bruno affected Leibniz' thought, there is no evidence whatever. What we have is a statement which bears strong superficial resemblances to the statement of Leibniz; the arguments, such as they are, the steps which lead up to the statement, are not similar. Leibniz' arguments are sufficiently strong not to demand support from the fact that there were monadologists before Leibniz. To his imagination we may concede plagiarism. But it is with the sources of his thought, not with the sources of his imagery, that we are concerned.

The other sources mentioned may be dismissed in the same way. It is interesting, perhaps, but not valuable, to observe that Leibniz read with appreciation a book by Maimonides. And though he never couples the names of Spinoza and Maimonides together, the notes which he made upon this book single out just the points of resemblance to the *Theologico-politicus* — the first work of Spinoza that he read. He was interested in Hebrew and Arabic studies. Bossuet sends to him for a translation of the Talmud. He announces to Bossuet a translation of the Koran. A dialogue of 1676 shows that he knew, through Maimonides, the doctrines of the Averrhoists and of a certain Jewish sect, the Motekallem. In 1687, while traveling in Bavaria, he undertook

* For Bruno, see H. Brunnhofer: *G. Brunos Lehre vom Kleinsten.* For Maimonides, see Foucher de Careil: *Leibniz, la philosophie juive*; Rubin: *Erkenntnistheorie Maimons.*

some study of the Kabbala, and perhaps noticed the theory of emanation from an infinite being which consists in an indivisible point — and the microcosm is said to be a familiar idea in Jewish philosophy. These studies, rather shallow it is true, illustrate Leibniz' insatiable curiosity toward every sort of theological hocus-pocus. Monadism was probably a satisfaction of this side of Leibniz' mind, as well as the outcome of his logical and meta-physical thought.

Of influences of suggestion, there is only one which may have been of the first importance — the influence of Plato, to be treated later. The main influences which directed Leibniz are of three kinds: the scholastic Aristotelian tradition in which he was brought up, the very early stimulus of a personal teacher toward a mathematical conception of the universe, and Leibniz' tem-porary adhesion to atomism. His chief motives, more or less cor-responding to this classification, were theological, logical, and physical.

Merz expresses the conventional opinion in saying that the *De principio individui* 'bears testimony to the young author's ex-tensive knowledge of scholastic learning as well as to his dexterity in handling their dialectical methods.'* I am incompetent to impugn the scholastic erudition of young Leibniz, but a perusal of this document impels me to exclaim with Kabitz, 'as if the copious citation of passages from scholastic compendia proved any "astonishing" learning on the part of Leibniz; as if he could not obtain these quotations just as well second-hand!'** The treatise is very short and very dull. Two or three passages in it are often quoted. 'Pono igitur: omne individuum sua tota entitate in-dividuatur';*** and 'Sed si omnis intellectus creatus tolleretur, illa relatio periret, et tamen res individuarentur, ergo tunc se ipsis.'**** The principle of individuation is not mental, nor is it

* Merz, p. 15.

** Kabitz, *Die Philosophie des jungen Leibniz*, p. 50.

*** 'I propose therefore that every individual thing is made individual by its own whole being.'

**** 'But if every intellect in creation were taken away, that relationship would perish; yet even so things would be made individual, and therefore in that event by themselves.'

negative. Though Leibniz documents this work with such names as Occam, Scotus, Aquinas, Suarez, Molina, Zabarella, what the thesis shows is not extent of learning or originality of thought. It shows that there was a certain body of inheritance which pointed in a certain direction. It shows a scholastic point of view from which Leibniz never really escaped, and which he never wholly rejected.* In the light of these quotations is to be interpreted not only monadism, but the materialistic atomism which for a time engaged his attention. At this early period, and indeed throughout his life, there is little evidence of direct adaptations from Aristotle. But here as always one finds the acceptance of the problem of substance, transmitted from Aristotle through the form which the school had given it. In some ways diametrically in opposition with Aristotle, this scholastic view of substance which Leibniz held is yet an Aristotelian inheritance. This point is of capital importance.

It appears that Leibniz abandoned his study of the philosophers of the church when he felt called, at a very early age, 'to adopt the mechanical view of nature. . . .'** But there was never a complete renunciation, and Leibniz, who seldom spoke ill of a dead philosopher, always praises the schoolmen. The change was a transition and not an apostasy. In 1663, at Jena, while pursuing his studies in jurisprudence, he fell under the influence of Weigel. Weigel was acquainted with the work of Copernicus, Kepler, and Galileo. Kabitz says that 'the fundamental conception of Leibniz' system according to which the universe is an harmonic, mathematico-logical related whole . . . became a firm conviction with Leibniz through Weigel, before he was acquainted with the work of Hobbes.'*** Bisterfeld of Leyden is another mathematician admired by Leibniz in his youth, and his influence is supposed to be visible in the *Arte Combinatoria.* The idea of a harmony

---

* Nolen, *Quid L. Aristoteli debuerit*, p. 27, quotes Leibniz as follows: 'Mea doctrina de substantia composita videtur esse ipsa doctrina scholae peripateticae. Nisi quod ille monadas non agnovit.' ('My doctrine of substance seems to be derived from the doctrine of substance of the peripatetic school, except that the latter was ignorant of monads.')

** Merz, p. 15.   *** Kabitz, *op. cit.*, p. 112.

of a universe of individual substances is present in other writings of Leibniz' adolescence.

Leibniz' scholastic training in metaphysics under Thomasius was followed by that period in which, as he says, 'when I had freed myself from the yoke of Aristotle [by which he means the attenuated scholasticism of his day], I took to the void and the atoms, for that is the view which best satisfies the imagination.'* This may have been about 1666.** It is easy to see from the *De principio individui* (written, according to his own chronology, when he had already fallen under the influence of Gassendi) that this liberation was merely a development of extreme nominalism in the currents of his time. In 1676 he can still write, 'Ego magis magisque persuasus sum de corporibus insecabilibus . . . simplicissima esse debent ac proinde sphaerica,' but goes on to say 'Nullus enim locus est tam parvus quin fingi possit esse in eo sphaeram ipso minorem. Ponamus hoc ita esse, nullus erit locus assignabilis vacuus. Et tamen Mundus erit plenus, unde intelligitur quantitatem inassignabilem esse aliquid.'*** The atomism survives in 1676, although the void is abandoned, and the influence of his mathematical work is visible (this was just at the end of the period in Paris, when he was corresponding with Newton through the medium of Oldenburg). In this year occurred also his visit to London and to the Hague.

In the next period of his life, when he had for some years been occupied chiefly with mathematical matters, falls the elaboration of his argument against Descartes's theory of matter — Descartes, who had been partly responsible for Leibniz' tendency toward a mechanical view. The unsatisfactory character of the views of Descartes and of Gassendi had, it is true, been pointed out by Leibniz several years before. In this later period, besides physics and pure mathematics, a third scientific interest may be noted. He

* Latta, p. 300.   ** See Kabitz, p. 53.
*** Couturat, 1903, p. 10. ('I am more and more convinced about indivisible particles . . . they must be very simple and therefore spherical. For there is no place so small that it would be impossible to imagine in it a sphere smaller than itself. We therefore propose the following: no assignable place shall be empty. And yet the Universe shall be full, from which it is understood that an unassignable quantity is still something.')

refers often to Swammerdam, Leuwenhoek, and Malpighi, and it is evident that he felt a genuine enthusiasm for the progress of biology, aside from the support which certain theories lent to his doctrine of preformation. But as his interest in biology is apparently subsequent to the observable beginnings of monadism, these theories were rather a confirmation than a stimulus.

To these philosophical and scientific occupations must be joined another which was no less important. This is his perfectly genuine passion for theology. Developed perhaps out of his early training, this theology, in a mind which never lost an interest it had once taken up, remained a powerful influence throughout his life. His solicitude for the orthodoxy of his philosophy was not merely policy or timidity; his theological disputations are not merely a cover for logical problems. Leibniz' theological motive is responsible for much of the psychology of his monads; it took deep root in his system, though not altogether without disturbance of the soil. The only two interpretations of Leibniz which are of any importance, that of Dillmann* and the superior interpretation of Russell and Couturat, minimize the significance of this motive.

'Ma métaphysique est toute mathématique, pour dire ainsi, ou la pourroit devenir,' Leibniz writes to the Marquis de l'Hôpital (Dec. 27, 1694). And Russell says in speaking of the subject-object relation, 'the whole doctrine depends, throughout, upon this purely logical tenet.'** Strictly speaking, this assertion is perfectly justified. For a historical account, it is insufficient. Leibniz puts his problems into logical form, and often converts them slyly into logical problems, but his prejudices are not always prejudices of logic. The value of Leibniz' logic is to a certain extent separable from the value of his philosophy. The view of the nature of substance with which he starts is due to a logical problem. But there is no logical descent from pluralism to the view that the ego is substance. Leibniz' view of substance is derived from Aristotle, but his *theory* of substance is different: it is Aristotle's theory filtered through scholasticism and tinctured by atomism and theology.

When we father the problem of substance upon Aristotle, we

* *Neue Darstellung der Leibnizischen Monadenlehre.*　　　** Russell, p. 49.

must remember that it was a problem which he never succeeded in resolving, or pretended to have resolved. The chief inheritance of modern philosophy from his doctrine is the proposition that 'substance is that which is not predicated of a subject, but of which all else is predicated' (*Metaphysica Z* 1029a 8–9). Aristotle recognizes that there are various senses in which we may use the term, and various substances besides the sensible substances, which have matter. In one sense, the composite of form and matter (e.g., animals and plants) is substance; in another sense substance is 'the form by which the matter is some definite thing' (1041b 8). And again the substratum (1028b 36–37) is that of which everything is predicated. Matter certainly is not substance, because matter has neither limit nor the potency of limit by separation (see Δ 1017b 1–8). And again the universal is more substantial than the particulars (H1042a 13–15). Wherever Aristotle pursues the concept of substance, it eludes him. These tentative definitions, assumed for dialetic purposes, are abandoned in favour of that of 1041b 27-31. This bears, it is true, very striking resemblances to the substance of Leibniz. As to the meaning of form and the relation of formal to efficient and final cause, Aristotle remains difficult and vague, while for Leibniz the formal and efficient causes in the case of substance are identical.

There is another and very serious difficulty in the theory of Aristotle. From one of Aristotle's points of view only the individual should be real, from the other only the specific. The form is always ἄτομον (indivisible); thought analyses and resynthesizes its constituents to give the λόγος τοῦ τί ἦν εἶναι (the reason for a thing being what it is). Of the subject, either the whole or a part of the definition can be affirmed: thus we can define Socrates *qua* man as ζῷον δίπουν λογικόν (a rational two-footed animal). But predications of particular individuals belong to the attributive, not to the definitory, type of judgment. In this type of judgment the predicate affirmed, although it belongs to the subject, is not a constituent of the subject's essential nature. As the essential nature of Socrates is man, anything which is not contained in the form of man in general will be attributive only and not definitory, inasmuch as it might have been otherwise. For Aristotle, not all predicates are contained in their subjects. Hence there can be no definition of individuals of a species (1039*b* 27–30). The substance must be individual, in order to be the subject; it must be a 'this.' But the 'this' cannot be composed of universals, because no number of 'suches' will constitute a 'this', and on the other hand it cannot be composed of other substances. We thus get two opposed views: the substance is the form of the species, in which case it breaks loose from the concrete thing and gives rise to the same difficulties which Aristotle censured in Plato; or the substance is the individual thing, in which case there is no definition and no knowledge. One view is in harmony with Aristotle's methodology, the other with his theory of elementary cognition.*

Aristotle is here betrayed by his representation theory — the exact correspondence between constituents of propositions and constituents of things; although in other contexts he is an epistemological monist. The same incoherence appears in his account of the soul. Is the substance the compound of matter and form, or the form alone?

It was the Aristotelian problem of substance, affected by scholasticism, that Leibniz took upon his shoulders at the beginning of his career. Later in life he observes that he has been re-reading Aristotle, and that he finds much of value in him. The extent of his acquaintance with the text may be left in doubt. It is probable that he had little or no direct knowledge, that he abandoned the study of the history of philosophy almost altogether for some years, and the fresh approach to Aristotle did not produce much effect upon his subsequent work. The interest lies in Leibniz' saturation which the Aristotelian tradition — in spite of a momentary peevishness against the degenerate scholasticism in which he had been brought up — and in the compound to which the contact of this training with the speculations of contemporary science give rise. To this particular problem the drawing of parallels and the estimating of borrowings — conscious and uncon-

* In *An. post.* Book II (Chap. XIX) 100*a* 15–17 we are told how the knowledge of the universals arises through experience of particulars. 'First principles' are arrived at by induction. What is not made clear is the status of the particulars after scientific knowledge is established.

scious — is irrelevant. Nor are we here concerned with the question whether 'this seemingly fantastic system could be deduced from a few simple premisses.'* The question is the actual genesis of the system. If, at the age of fifteen, Leibniz inclined to the view that substances are particular individuals and that relations exist only in the mind; if we can see that his transition to atomic materialism follows quite easily from this; if we find that his further development depended upon the way in which his scientific researches and his theological prejudices — largely an inheritance from his early training — played into each other; then we shall conclude that his metaphysics and his scientific achievements — logical and mathematical — are two different values.

What is curious about Leibniz' mind is the existence of two distinct currents. As a scientist he has a clear and consistent development. Every step is justified and coherent from this point of view alone. His metaphysics is carefully built upon his scientific evolution. On the other side is a strong devotion to theology. His study of Descartes marks a stage in the development of both. Descartes's theory of matter, and Descartes's theory of self-consciousness both had their effect upon him. And it is always the same mind working, clear and cold, the mind of a doctor of the church. He is nearer to the Middle Ages, nearer to Greece, and yet nearer to us, than are men like Fichte and Hegel.

We have seen that there is a very great difference between the Aristotelian theory of substance and the nominalism deriving from it with which Leibniz starts. Both in the *Metaphysica* and in the *De anima*, it is true, Aristotle leaves the answer somewhat ambiguous. When he discusses the substance of organic beings we are apt to think that each individual is a substance — that the form of each body is an individual — one form for Socrates, and another for Callias. It is difficult to avoid this conclusion, but in general, for Aristotle as well as for Plato, whatever was merely individual was perishable and incapable of being a subject of knowledge. But if we say, with Burnet** that 'Plato found reality, whether intelligible or sensible, in the combination of matter and form and

* Russell, p. viii.　　** *Greek Philosophy*, p. 331-2.

not in either separately,' and take the same view of Aristotle, yet we cannot say that they found it in each individual as a world apart. This is an instance of the differences between Leibniz and the Greeks. In Leibniz we find the genesis of a psychological point of view; ideas tend to become particular mental facts, attributes of particular substances. If the form or principle of Aristotle were different in each man, this form would be Leibniz' soul. For the Greek the human was the typically human, individual differences were not of scientific interest; for the modern philosopher individual differences were of absorbing importance.

We may now trace the two currents which are imperfectly united in the monad. Leibniz approaches the problem of substance primarily as a physicist. 'Leibniz does not begin with the problem, what is the substance of the body, what is its origin, but from this: how the principle of the body itself may be conceived.'* To those readers — there are still a few — who know Leibniz only through the *Monadology*, the steps to the conclusion will remain unknown. Unless we appreciate the original question we shall be unable to understand his solution of the problem of body and soul, and of the problem of our knowledge of external objects. He never asked the question, 'do physical bodies exist?' but always, 'what is the principle which makes physical bodies intelligible?' The answer is found in his reaction to Cartesianism. And at this point, while the problem of energy was engaging his attention, he read some of the dialogues of Plato, and was confirmed in his conclusions especially by certain parts of the *Sophist*. What we get is on the one hand an explanation of the principle of matter, and on the other an idealistic metaphysic, largely influenced by Descartes, based upon self-consciousness. The latter aspect has of course been more exploited than the former.

Leibniz' account of physical matter is a much more scientific, but in some respects much cruder, explanation than Aristotle's. For Aristotle's account is fundamentally a relativistic one, i.e., 'matter' has various meanings in relation to shifting points of view which form a series but are not themselves defined. There

* Dillman, p. 63.

are meanings in various contexts, but no absolute meaning; and
the series of points of view, the series of contexts, has no absolute
meaning either. One misses the whole point of Aristotle's theory
if one regards matter as a 'thing'. It is — whether as primitive
matter, as the four elements, or as any compounds (I mean
συνθέσεις (syntheses, compositions) not μίξεις (mixtures)) of any
degree of complexity formed out of these — one side of a contrast in
the mind (or imposed upon the mind) though this mind is no more
absolutely definable than matter itself. (Hence Aristotle is
neither an idealist, in the modern sense, nor a pragmatist.)
Materia prima is not simply negative nor is it positive in any apprehensible way. It is simply the furthest possible extension of
meaning of a concept which has arisen out of practical complexes.
The next stage in the conception of matter, it will be recollected,
is that of a subject possessing two out of two pairs of opposites
(wet-dry, hot-cold). The *materia prima* is not *actual*, because it has
no predicates; the smallest number of predicates which an actual
existent can have is two. That is, whatever is merely hot, or merely
dry, is not a substance but is identical with the quality itself; but
whatever is hot and wet, or cold and dry, is a substance different
from its predicates. These elements — the possible combinations
of four qualities — are capable of transmutation into one another
in a cycle which occurs in the exchange of qualities (the hot-dry
becomes hot-wet, the hot-wet becomes wet-cold, etc.). The third
stage of matter is that of the stable compounds of the four elements held together in various proportions. This progress is not
a chemical theory in the modern sense; it is a series of points of
view. The formal cause is therefore identical with the thing itself,
and whether the form is there is a question of what we regard as
the thing. The lump of marble is a σωρός (pile, heap) of higher
compounds of the four elements — or it is a statue. One must
keep in mind the two apparently inconsistent propositions: (1)
there are no forms of individuals,* (2) the form and the matter
compose one whole.

* Except of course eternal and unique individuals, like the moon, which is the
only individual of its species. And for later theology, the angels.

The Development of Leibniz' Monadism

Aristotle is too keen a metaphysician to start from a naive view of matter or from a one-sided spiritualism. To a certain extent Leibniz keeps this middle ground too. But his metaphysics tends to fall apart, as the result of his inherited nominalism, and the fissure between his scientific and his theological interests. Starting as a physicist, Leibniz naturally assumes that matter is not a relative term but that it is (if it exists at all, of which he has no doubt) something absolute. The substantiality of matter consists then (after his defection from Cartesianism) in the concept of force. Force is not conceived as something behind matter, which could be actual without matter. But neither is it a 'form' in quite the Aristotelian sense. The 'real and animated point' of the *Système nouveau* is from an Aristotelian point of view merely another individual, or a form of an individual. It is purely and simply a physical explanation. It involves no theory of knowledge, because it does not take into account the point of view of an observer; it is a contrast not between matter and form, but between a particular substance and its states.

Leibniz' distinction between *materia prima* and *materia secunda* (of bodies) is superficially Aristotelian. But it is really only a distinction between two ways in which matter may be considered for the purposes of the physicist. It is a distinction of uses and not of contexts. 'Matter' is not a relative term. The ancient distinction between matter and form does not correspond to the modern distinction, since Descartes, of matter and spirit. And the dichotomy is as strongly marked in Leibniz as in Descartes. His solution of the difficulty marks the wide gulf that separates modern from ancient philosophy. For Aristotle matter and form were always relative, but never identical. For Leibniz matter and spirit are absolute reals, but are really (as for Spinoza) the same thing. The difference for Leibniz is that between internal and external aspects. *Materia prima* is not a stage, it is an external aspect, and even for physics he finds this aspect insufficient. He is therefore led gradually into a metaphysical conception. But from this metaphysical account of the nature of the physical universe to his doctrine of souls there is really no legitimate inference.

The Development of Leibniz' Monadism

The theory of forces, as the substances of which material changes are the states, is not the theory of the soul which derives from his more theological interest. It is, as we have said, simply an analysis of the physical universe. Had Leibniz been quite consistent he would have gone on to explain organic and conscious activity on a strictly physical basis. This he did accomplish in some measure. His doctrine of expression* is an account of perception consistent with a purely physical and mathematical point of view. But his transmigration** of human souls is muddled by the identification of soul, in the sense of personality, with the animated point; of the core of feeling of the self with the force of which it is predicated. From his physical point of view he cannot arrive at self-consciousness, so that his doctrine of force has two grounds — the theory of dynamics and the *feeling* of activity. If we refuse to consider self-consciousness a simple and single act, if making an object of oneself merely means the detachment and observation of particular states by other states, then the 'force' slips out of our hands altogether. It remains 'internal', it is true, in contrast with primary matter, but its internality is not a character of self-consciousness. And in this event the whole theory becomes completely naturalistic. Something is the subject, but it is not the *I* which I know, or which anybody knows. And there then remains no reason why we should longer maintain a plurality of subjects. Force becomes one. Against such a conclusion Leibniz was set, (1) because it ceases to have any value for physics, and (2) because it interferes with our claim for personal immortality. Theology and physics join forces (so to speak) to rob metaphysics of its due.

Hence two curious difficulties arise. An animated force, a monad, tends to become an animated atom. The monad exerts its activity at a point in space and time. Artefacts, as for Aristotle, are merely groups of monads without a dominant monad. Organic bodies are groups with a dominant monad. In the latter case, in

* See Letter to Arnauld, Oct. 6, 1687.
** Leibniz of course explicitly repudiates any 'transmigration' of monads. But when he comes to the human soul its adventures seem to be tantamount to this.

the case of a human being, in what sense is my body *mine*, since it is also the bodies of other monads? The dominant monad should be the form of the body, instead of which it bears a strong resemblance to a larger or more powerful cell, and the soul would have to be located, like Descartes's, in a particular place. Russell, in contrasting Leibniz' two conflicting theories says of the second view: 'in the other theory, mind and body together make one substance, making a true unity.'* So they ought to do. If the mind cannot make the body into a *unum per se*, instead of a mere aggregate, the original physical theory has advanced to a point at which mind and body fall apart. The second view appears to descend from Aristotle.** The first appears to descend from atomism. From neither philosophy does Leibniz ever shake himself quite free.

There is, from the physical side, a sense in which the monad is truly immortal. Force is indestructible, and will continue in various manifestations. But force in this sense is entirely impersonal. We cannot conceive of its persistence except by associating it with particular particles of matter. Leibniz is led by his difficulties almost to the point of either denying the existence of matter altogether, or else setting up a sort of matter which will be something real besides monads.

The second objection is connected with the generation and destruction of life. For Aristotle some account of generation and destruction is rendered possible by his provisional distinction between efficient and formal causes. Aristotle was not embarrassed by a belief in personal immortality, and his philosophy confines itself with fair success to an examination of the actual, the present life. But Leibniz' force is indestructible in a different sense from Aristotle's form.*** It persists in time as a particular existence. The monad which is myself must have previously existed; it must have

* Russell, p. 150.

** Leibniz actually says (letter to Arnauld, July 14, 1686): 'The soul is nevertheless the form of the body.'

*** Aristotle and Plato, I am inclined to believe, owe their success in navigating between the particular and the universal, the concrete and the abstract, largely to the fact that 'forms', 'species', had to the Greek mind not exactly the same meaning as for us. They were concrete without being particular.

been one of the monads composing the body of father or mother.*
This theory has the disadvantages of practically denying the independence of mind from body and of separating monadhood
from selfhood. It substitutes biological behaviour for conscious
activity.

Commencing with an analysis of the nature of matter, Leibniz
is led to the view of a universe consisting of centres of force. From
this point of view the human soul is merely one of these forces, and
its activity should be reducible to physical laws. Under the influence of an Aristotelian doctrine of substance, he comes to
conclusions which are not at all Aristotelian, by his nominalistic
assumption that substances are particulars. From a materialistic
atomism he is led to a spiritualistic atomism. In this he shows
again an important difference between the ancient and the modern
world. It is illustrated in the prejudice of Aristotle against the
differences between individuals of the same species which he as-
cribes to the perverse and unaccountable influence of matter. To
the Greek, this variety of points of view would seem a positive
evil; as a theory of knowledge, it would seem a refuge of scepti-
cism; to Leibniz and the modern world, it enhances the interest
of life. And yet the view of Leibniz comes, *via* nominalism, out of
Aristotle himself.

From the point of view of physics we have a consistent explanation which represents a great advance upon crude materialism.
But it is difficult to retain the separate forces unless we conceive
of matter as a positive principle of individuation. Not that the
doctrine of activity and passivity is wholly unsatisfactory.** Its
effect is to reduce causality to function. And but for the Aristotelian influence, it might possibly have done so. Instead of monads
we might then have had atomic particulars. But Leibniz sometimes confuses the mathematico-physical and the historical points
of view. It is true that the future of the monad should be theoreti-

* Russell, p. 154.
** There are implicitly two views of activity and passivity. According to one,
causality is a useful way of treating natural phenomena. According to the other,
here is true activity in clear perception, true passivity in confused. This illustrates
the mixture of motives.

cally predictable. But Leibniz leaves the basis of prediction uncertain. Without recourse to mysticism, the reasons why a monad should pass from the unconscious to the conscious state, why one of the monads composing the body of father or mother should suddenly be elected to domination over a new body of monads, remain unsolved. We have seen that the notion of soul or spirit is not to be reached by the theory of monads as an explanation of the principle of matter. If it is part of Leibniz' inheritance we may inquire just what Aristotle's view of the soul was.

Leibniz' theory of soul is, like that of Descartes, derived from scholasticism. It is very remote from that of either Plato, Aristotle, or Plotinus. For the Greeks, even for Plotinus, the soul is a substance in a sense which does not include personal immortality. For Aristotle there is no continuity between the stages of soul, between vegetable, animal, and human life. And the definition of monads as 'points of view' is, so far as I can see, entirely modern.

For Aristotle, according to his own explicit statement, there is no 'soul' in general. As the species of figure to figure in general, so are the souls of various species of animal to 'soul' in general.[*] In the higher grades of soul the same functions persist, but in a form altered by the nature of the whole. The organs of different species are related by analogy — as root is to plant, so mouth is to animal, but mouth is not a development of root. The *De anima* is not so much a psychological as a biological treatise. We find in the animal the τροφή (nourishment) and αὔξησις (growth) of the plant, but completely altered in the addition of a new faculty — αἴσθησις (perception). And these faculties are not sharp dividing lines, but in the ascending scale are used more and more loosely.[**] The natural species are immutable, and the difference does not consist in addition or subtraction of faculty.

There is a suggestion, but only a suggestion, of the doctrine of Aristotle in the three classes of monads. Even the lowest class of

[*] *De Anima*, Book II, 414b, 20 ff.
[**] Cf. Book II, 413b, 12–13; 414a, 31 ff; and Book III, 432a, 15 ff. Motion according to 413b, 13, is not a fourth species of the soul besides θρεπτικόν αἰσθητικόν, διανοητικόν (the principles of growth, perception, and thought).

monad has appetition.* The second has feeling (sentiment) which is something more than αἴσθησις (perception) and includes φαντασία (imagination) and perhaps διάνοια (thought). The soul of man only has self-consciousness, a knowledge of eternal and necessary truths — νοῦς (mind). It seems very probable that this scheme was suggested by Aristotle** but there is a profound difference. The classification of Aristotle is on the basis of biological functions. These are functions of the organism as a whole, a complex substance. Plants are not ζῷα (animals), and have no appetition. Aristotle makes much of the distinction between beings which are attached to a single place and those which move about. For Leibniz the distinction is not biological, but psychological, and is everywhere a difference of degree. The lower monads, if they had clearer perceptions, would rise in the scale. It is not a limitation of the body, but a limitation of the nature of the monad itself which establishes differences. For Leibniz the series is a continuum; for Aristotle it is not. For Leibniz desire characterizes mind; for Aristotle desire is always of the complex organism; the function of mind is solely the apprehension of the eternal and necessary truths and principles.

There is another point upon which Leibniz may have drawn his inspiration from Aristotle, and that is the 'common sense'. 'The ideas which are said to come from more than one sense, like those of space, figure, motion, rest, are rather from common sense, that is from the mind itself, for they are ideas of the pure understanding, but they are related to the external, and the senses make us perceive them.'*** Leibniz' theory appears to be a transition between Aristotle and Kant. What Aristotle says is this: 'The above [i.e., colour, sound, etc.] are called qualities which belong to the respective senses; the perceptions common to all are motion, rest, number, figure, magnitude. These are not *propria* of any, but are common to all.'**** Whereas Leibniz stuffs these κοινά (common qualities) into the mind, Aristotle goes no farther than to say

* *Monadology*, 19.
** And, in passing, it seems possible that the theory of Leibniz may have supplied a hint for the romantic evolutionism of Diderot.
*** Russell, p. 163.   **** *De Anima*, Book II, 418a, 17 ff.

that they are perceived κατὰ συμβεβηκός (accidentally) by all the senses. There is not, as is sometimes thought, a 'common sense' which apprehends them, as the eye perceives colour.* What is interesting in the present context is the cautious empiricism of Aristotle's theory, contrasted with the more daring but less sound speculations of Leibniz.

The question of the relation of mind to matter is handled by Leibniz differently from either Aristotle or Spinoza. I am inclined to think that it was conceived quite independently of Spinoza. Leibniz attacks Spinoza fiercely on the ground of Spinoza's naturalism, and for his disbelief in free-will and immortality.** He perceives, quite correctly, that Spinoza's view of the relation of mind and body leads to a materialistic epiphenominalism. 'With Spinoza the reason does not possess ideas, it is an idea.' He insists that the mind and the body are not the same thing, any more than the principle of action and the principle of passion are the same thing. But he inclines to believe that the difference between mind and matter is a difference of degree, that in all created monads there is materiality. (There seems to be a relation between *materia prima* of monads and *materia prima* of matter.) Now this suggests the Aristotelian relativity of matter and form; for Aristotle the higher substances are more 'formed', the percentage of crude matter seems to decrease. There is no matter and no form in an absolute sense (except the form of God, who is rather a disturbing factor). But whereas for Aristotle matter exists only in contrast with form, and formed matter may be the matter for a higher form, for Leibniz matter really exists independently of spirit, but is really spirit.

Leibniz' use of the term 'entelechy' is not identical with that of Aristotle. The monad is called entelechy apparently because it is complete in itself, complete in the sense of self-sufficient; while the entelechy of Aristotle is the *completion* or actuality of something. In the *De anima* the soul is called the first entelechy of body

---

* Zabarella, probably the greatest of all Aristotelian commentators, is very positive on this point.

** See Foucher de Careil: *Réfutation inédite de Spinoza par Leibniz.*

To be strictly consistent, Aristotle should perhaps have held that soul is the second entelechy, since he maintains that it is only actual when it energizes; but he is merely trying to distinguish between the form and its operation.* Entelechy means that the body would not be a human body without the soul. It is difficult, it is true, not to think of the soul as something added to the body (as to Galatea) or else to identify soul with the (living) body. Soul is to body as cutting is to the axe: realizing itself in its actions, and not completely real when abstracted from what it does. In the light of Aristotle's elaborate critique of earlier theories of the soul, his view is seen as an attempt to get away from the abstractions of materialism or of spiritualism with which we begin. For Aristotle reality is here and now; and the true nature of mind is found in the activity which it exercises. Attempt to analyse the mind, as a thing, and it is nothing. It is an operation. Aristotle's psychology therefore starts with psycho-physics, and ascends to speculative reason. It is only then that we perceive what mind is, and in retrospect find that it was present in the simplest sensation.

The word entelechy as used by Leibniz loses the meaning which it had for Aristotle. It becomes figurative and unimportant. Leibniz appears at first less a dichotomist than either Aristotle or Descartes. In effect, the breach between mind and matter becomes far wider than in the system of Aristotle. In order that mind may persist at all times as something distinct from the body, appeal is made to the subconscious, — a parallelism even more mystifying than that of Spinoza. With Leibniz the relation of mind and matter is closer, the relation of body and soul more remote, than with Aristotle. The weakness in Leibniz' theory of body and soul may be due to two causes. On the one hand his theological bias made separation of body and soul essential; and on the other hand it was necessary, for his more strictly philosophical argument, that the monads should persist after the compound substances, the bodies, which are their points of view. It

* See *De anima*, Book II, 412a, 28, where δυνάμει ζωὴν ἔχοντος means having 'the potentiality of functioning', not 'the potentiality of soul'. The above distinction between form and operation was pointed out by Zabarella.

is required both by his theory of substance, and by his demand for a mathematical metaphysic. The causal series which is the monad should apparently have no last term.* Perception (in Leibniz' general statement of expression) requires that every series should be similar both to every other series and to the series of series.** The same theory which demands unconscious perception seems to demand also a series which shall not terminate in time. Supposing that the destruction of individual monads shall leave the total, as an infinite number, undiminished, nevertheless the monad as a substance will have to shut up shop, and we shall be left with a number of relations relating nothing. Some sort of persistence is necessary for the system, though not the personal immortality which Leibniz is interested in supporting. It is evident that with the possibility of changes of 'points of view' the meaning of prediction becomes hopelessly attenuated. Every moment will see a new universe. At every moment there will be a new series of series; but continuity makes necessary a point of view from which there shall be a permanent series of series of series.

Leibniz' theory of mind and matter, of body and soul, is in some ways the subtlest that has ever been devised. Matter is an arrested moment of mind, 'mind without memory.'*** By state is not meant feeling, but the monad at any instant of time.**** In many ways it is superior to that of Aristotle. When he turns to preformation, to the *vinculum substantiale*, to the immortality of the soul, we feel a certain repulsion; for with all the curious fables of the *Timaeus* or the *Physics* and Aristotle's history of animals, we know that Aristotle and Plato were somehow more secure, better balanced, and less superstitious than the man who was in power of intellect their equal.

There are two other points in monadism which direct attention to the Greeks. These are the theory of innate ideas and the theory

---

* See Russell: 'Recent work on the philosophy of Leibniz,' *Mind*, Vol. XI (1903) pp. 199–200.

** See *ibid.*, p. 199.

*** Quoted from *Theoria motus abstracti*, 1671 by Latta, p. 230 n. Compare the Bergsonian theory of matter as consciousness 'running down'.

**** Cf. 'only indivisible monads and their states are absolutely real.'

of substance as force expressed in the 'Sophist'. So far as the question of indebtedness goes I think that the answer is clear enough. The views which Leibniz held were urged upon him by his own premises. He undoubtedly read Plato at a time when his own theory was not yet crystallized, but he cannot be said to have borrowed. He may be given full credit for having restored to life in a new form the doctrines of Plato and Aristotle. The monad is a reincarnation of the form which is the formal cause of Aristotle. But it is also more and less. The outstanding difference is that he sets out from an investigation of *physical* force, and his monads tend to become atomic centres of force, particular existences. Hence a tendency to psychologism, to maintain that ideas always find their home in particular minds, that they have a psychological as well as a logical existence. Leibniz on this side opened the way for modern idealism. To his anticipations of modern logic of a school opposed to absolute idealism, it is unnecessary for me to point. No philosophy contains more various possibilities of development, no philosophy unites more various influences. That he did not always unite them successfully — that he never quite reconciled modern physics, medieval theology, and Greek substance — is not to be reproved when we consider the magnitude of his task and the magnitude of his accomplishment.

Leibniz' Monads and Bradley's Finite Centres*

No philosopher is more fantastic than Leibniz in presentation, few have been less intelligently interpreted. At first sight, none is less satisfactory. Yet Leibniz remains to the end disquieting and dangerous. He represents no one tradition, no one civilization; he is allied to no social or literary tendency; his thought cannot be summed up or placed. Spinoza represents a definite emotional attitude; suggestive as he is, his value can be rated. Descartes is a classic, and is dead. 'Candide' is a classic: Voltaire was a wise man, and not dangerous. Rousseau is not a classic, nor was he a wise man; he has proved an eternal source of mischief and inspiration. Reviewing the strange opinions, almost childish in *naiveté*, of birth and death, of body and soul, of the relation between vegetable and animal, of activity and passivity — together with the pitiful efforts at orthodoxy and the cautious ethics of this German diplomat, together with his extraordinary facility of scientific insight, one is disconcerted at the end. His orthodoxy is more alarming than others' revolution, his fantastic guesses more enduring than others' rationality.

Beside the work of Russell and of Couturat I have found only one author of assistance in attempting to appreciate the thought of Leibniz. In Bradley's *Appearance and Reality* I seemed to find features strikingly similar to those of monadism. So that re-reading Leibniz I cannot help thinking that he was the first to express, perhaps half unconsciously, one of those fundamental varieties of

* Reprinted from *The Monist* XXVI (October 1916) 566–76. Translations have been added for this edition.

198

view which perpetually recur as novelties. With his motives, logical and otherwise, I am not here concerned. I only wish to point out, and leave for consideration, certain analogies.

That monadism begins with Leibniz I think will be conceded. It is characteristic of the man that everything about his monads, except the one essential point which makes them his own, he may have borrowed from an author with whom he was certainly acquainted. Bruno's theory has everything in common with that of Leibniz except this one point. A kind of pre-established harmony, the continuity of animal and vegetable and of organic and inorganic, the representation of the whole in the part, even the words *monadum monas* (the monad of monads): these points of identity one finds.* But the monad of Bruno has this difference: it has windows. And it is just the impenetrability of the Leibnizian monads which constitutes their originality and which seems to justify our finding a likeness between Leibniz and Bradley. In any case, there is no philosopher with whom the problem of sources is less important than with Leibniz. The fact that he could receive stimulation from such various sources and remain so independent of the thought of his own time** indicates both the robustness and the sensitiveness of genius. He had studied Thomas, and probably with great care the *Metaphysics* and the *De anima*, but he was not an Aristotelian; he was probably profoundly struck by the passage *Sophistes* 247e, but any one who has read his panegyric of the *Phaedo**** will probably agree that his praise is more the approval of posterity than the inter-

---

* See H. Brunnhofer, *G. Bruno's Lehre vom Kleinsten als die Quelle der praestabilierten Harmonie von Leibniz* (Leipsic, 1890), pp. 59–63, for quotations, e.g. from *De Triplici Minimo*: 'Deus est monadum monas.' Also from *Spaccio della bestia trionfante*: 'In ogni uomo, in ciascuno individuo si contempla un mondo, un universo.' Brunnhofer even traces the window metaphor back to the Song of Solomon: 'Prospiciens per fenestras.'

** At least he affirms his independence. In 1679 he writes to Malebranche that, as when he began to meditate he was not imbued with Cartesian opinions, he was led to 'entrer dans les choses par une autre porte et decouvrir de nouveaux pays.' He is also inclined to speak rather slightingly of Spinoza. See Wendt, Die *Entwickelung der Leibnizischen Monadenlehre bis zum Jahre 1695* (Berlin, 1886). The germs of monadism appear as early as 1663.

*** *Discourse on Metaphysics*, Chapter XXVI.

pretation of discipleship. Leibniz' originality is in direct, not inverse ratio to his erudition.

More than multiplicity of influences, perhaps the multiplicity of motives and the very occasional reasons for some of Leibniz' writings, make him a bewildering and sometimes ludicrous writer. The complication of his interests in physics, his interests in logic, and his equally genuine interest in theology, make his views a jungle of apparent contradictions and irrelevancies. His theory of physical energy, for example, leads to an unsound metaphysical theory of activity, and his solicitude for the preservation of human immortality leads to a view which is only an excrescence upon monadism,* and which is in every way less valuable than Aristotle's. Thus there are features of the theory which are inessential. When we confine our attention to the resemblances between Leibniz' and Bradley's views, we will find I think that they cover everything essential. These are (1) complete isolation of monads from each other; (2) sceptical theory of knowledge, relativistic theory of space, time, and relations, a form of antiintellectualism in both writers; from which follows (3) the indestructibility of the monads; (4) the important doctrine of 'expression'.** Certain distinctions of Bradley's, as the (relative) distinction between finite centres and selves, are also implicit in Leibniz. The relation of soul and body, the possibility of panpsychism, the knowledge of soul by soul, are problems which come to closely similar solutions in the two philosophies.

I suggest that from the 'pluralism' of Leibniz there is only a step to the 'absolute zero' of Bradley, and that Bradley's Absolute dissolves at a touch into its constituents.

In the first place, Leibniz' theory of degrees of perfection among monads approximates to a theory of degrees of reality. Mr Russell has pointed out how easy a step it would have been for Leibniz to have made reality the subject of all predicates. The world consists of simple substances and their states. The subject

---

* It leads Leibniz almost to the admission that persistence in the case of the lower types of monad is meaningless. Cf. *Discourse*, XXXIV.

** See Letter to Arnauld, Oct. 6, 1687.

is never, even from a timeless point of view, merely equivalent to the sum of its states; it is incapable of exhaustion by any addition of predicates. The question with which Leibniz attempted to cope in his first thesis, and the question which he was never able satisfactorily to settle, was what makes a real subject, what the principle of individuation is. Nowhere in the correspondence with Arnauld do we find a trustworthy mark of differentiation between substantial and accidental unities. If everything which can have predicates, everything which can be an object of attention, is a substance, the whole theory falls to the ground; but if this is not the case, we shall either be obliged to make reality the subject of all predicates, or we shall be forced to distinguish, as do some idealists, between judgments and pseudo-judgments, and the logical basis for monadism fails. If we cannot find by inspection an obvious and indubitable token of difference between the substantial and the accidental, we shall in the end find substantiality only in reality itself; or, what comes to the same thing, we shall find degrees of substantiality everywhere. In the latter case substance becomes relative to finite and changing points of view, and in the end again we must seek refuge in the one substance, or resign ourselves to find no refuge at all.

This omnipresence of substance, in degree, comes very near at times to being Leibniz' true doctrine. 'One thing expresses another, in my use of the term,' he says, 'when there is a constant and regulated relation between what can be said of the one and of the other. . . . Expression is common to all forms, and is a class of which ordinary perception, animal feeling, and intellectual knowledge are species. . . . Now, such expression is found everywhere, because all substances sympathize with one another and receive some proportional change corresponding to the slightest motion in the whole universe'; and further in the same letter 'you object that I admit substantial forms only in the case of animated bodies — a position which I do not, however, remember to have taken.'* We remark also that the lowest monads are in no very significant sense persistent: '[T]he result from a moral or practical

* To Arnauld, Oct. 6, 1687.

201

standpoint is the same as if we said that they perished in each case, and we can indeed say it from the physical standpoint in the same way that we say bodies perish in their dissolution.'* The permanence of these monads seems to assert itself in order to save a theory.

There is indeed a point of view, necessary even in the severest monism, from which everything, so far as it is an object, so far as it can be assigned predicates, is equally real. But if we recognize the relativity of the point of view for which reality is merely the fact of being an object from that point of view, then the only criterion of reality will be completeness and cohesion. Suppose that some of the objects from a point of view are not direct objects (things), but other points of view, then there is no phenomenal test of their reality, *qua* points of view. So far as we cannot treat them as things, the only objective criterion of the reality will be their perfection. In any system in which degrees of reality play a part, reality may be defined in terms of value, and value in terms of reality.

Leibniz does not succeed in establishing the reality of several substances. On the other hand, just as Leibniz' pluralism is ultimately based upon faith, so Bradley's universe, actual only in finite centres, is only by an act of faith unified. Upon inspection, it falls away into the isolated finite experiences out of which it is put together. Like monads they aim at being one; each expanded to completion, to the full reality latent within it, would be identical with the whole universe. But in so doing it would lose the actuality, the here and now, which is essential to the small reality which it actually achieves. The Absolute responds only to an imaginary demand of thought, and satisfies only an imaginary demand of feeling. Pretending to be something which makes finite centres cohere, it turns out to be merely the assertion that they do. And this assertion is only true so far as we here and now find it to be so.

It is as difficult for Bradley as for Leibniz to maintain that there is any world at all, to find any objects for these mirrors to mirror.

* *Discourse on Metaphysics*, Chapter XXXIV.

Leibniz' Monads and Bradley's Finite Centres

The world of both is ideal construction. The distinction between 'ideal' and 'real' is present to Leibniz as well as to Bradley. The former's theory of space is, like the latter's, relativistic, even qualitative.* Relations are the work of the mind.** Time exists only from finite points of view. Nothing is real, except experience present in finite centres. The world, for Bradley, is simply the *intending* of a world by several souls or centres. 'The world is such that we can make the same intellectual construction. We can, more or less, set up a scheme, in which every one has a place, a system constant and orderly, and in which the relations apprehended by each percipient coincide. . . . Our inner worlds, I may be told, are divided from each other, but the outer world of experience is common to all; and it is by standing on this basis that we are able to communicate. Such a statement would be incorrect. My external sensations are no less private to myself than are my thoughts or my feelings. In either case my experience falls within my own circle, a circle closed on the outside; and, with all its elements alike, every sphere is opaque to the others which surround it. With regard to communicability, there is in fact not any difference of kind, but only of degree. . . . [I]t is not true that our physical experiences have unity, in any sense which is inapplicable to the worlds we call internal. . . . In brief, regarded as an existence which appears in a soul, the whole world for each is peculiar and private to that soul. . . . No experience can lie open to inspection from outside; no direct guarantee of identity is possible. . . . The real identity of ideal content, by which all souls live and move, cannot work in common save by the path of external appearance.'***

Perhaps this is only a statement of a usual idealistic position, but never has it been put in a form so extreme. A writer to whose words Mr Bradley would probably subscribe, Professor Bosanquet, formulates the orthodox view: '[N]o phase in a particular con-

* See *Appearance*, p. 32; Letter to Arnauld, April 30, 1687.
** 'And as regards space and time, Leibniz always endeavoured to reduce them to attributes of the substances in them. Thus Leibniz is forced . . . to the Kantian theory that relations, though veritable, are the work of the mind.' Russell, p. 14.
*** *Appearance*, p. 304 ff.

sciousness is merely a phase of the apparent subject, but it is
always and essentially a member of a further whole of experience,
which passes through and unites the states of many consciousnesses. . . .* This view Mr Bradley also holds. But he more often
emphasizes the other aspect. Each finite centre is, 'while it lasts',
the whole world. The world of practice, the world of objects, is
constructed out of the ideal identities intended by various souls.

For Bradley, I take it, an object is a common intention of several
souls, cut out (as in a sense are the souls themselves) from immediate experience. The genesis of the common world can only
be described by admitted fictions, since in the end there is no question of its origin in time: on the one hand our experiences are
similar because they are of the same objects, and on the other hand
the objects are only 'intellectual constructions' out of various and
quite independent experiences. So, on the one hand, my experience
is in principle essentially public. My emotions may be better
understood by others than by myself; as my oculist knows my
eyes. And on the other hand everything, the whole world, is
private to myself. Internal and external are thus not adjectives
applied to different contents within the same world; they are
different points of view.

I will pass now to another consideration. Is the finite centre or
the soul the counterpart to the monad? It is very difficult to keep
the meanings of 'soul', 'finite centre', and 'self' quite distinct. All
are more or less provisional and relative. A self is an ideal and
largely a practical construction, one's own self as much as that of
others. My self 'remains intimately one thing with that finite
centre within which my universe appears. Other selves on the
contrary are for me ideal objects. . . .'** The self is a construction
in space and time. It is an object among others, a self among
others, and could not exist save in a common world. The soul (as
in the passage quoted at length) is almost the same as finite
centre. The soul, considered as finite centre,*** cannot be acted

* *Principle of Individuality and Value*, p. 315.
** *Truth and Reality*, p. 418.
*** 'A soul is a finite centre viewed as an object existing in time with a before
and after of itself,' *Ibid.*, p. 414.

upon by other entities, since a finite centre is a universe in itself. 'If you confine your attention to the soul as a soul, then every possible experience is no more than that which happens in and to this soul. You have to do with psychical events which qualify the soul, and in the end these events, so far as you are true to your idea, are merely states of the soul. Such a conception is for certain purposes legitimate and necessary. . . .'* Change, accordingly, cannot be due to any agency outside of these states themselves; it can only be, 'in every state of a substance, some element or quality in virtue of which that state is not permanent, but tends to pass into the next state. This element is what Leibniz means by activity.'**

The soul only differs from the finite centre in being considered as something not identical with its states. The finite centre, so far as I can pretend to understand it, *is* immediate experience. It is not in time, though we are more or less forced to think of it under temporal conditions. 'It comes to itself as all the world and not as one world among others. And it has properly no duration through which it lasts. It can contain a lapse and a before and after, but these are subordinate.'*** The finite centre in a sense contains its own past and future. 'It has, or it contains, a character, and on that character its own past and future depend.'**** This is more clearly the case with the soul. But it would be untrue to go on and declare that the soul 'bears traces' of everything that happens to it. It would be a mistake to go on, holding this view of the soul, and distinguish between various grades of soul according to faculty. This would be to confuse the soul which is a whole world, to which nothing comes except as its own attribute and adjective, with the soul which can be described by its way of acting upon an environment. In this way Leibniz thrusts himself into a nest of difficulties. The concepts of centre, of soul, and of self and personality must be kept distinct. The point of view from which each soul is a world in itself must not be confused with the point of view from which each soul is only the function of a

* *Ibid.*, p. 415. ** Russell, p. 45
*** *Truth and Reality*, p. 410 **** *Ibid.*, p. 411.

physical organism, a unity perhaps only partial, capable of alteration, development, having a history and a structure, a beginning
and apparently an end. And yet these two souls are the same. And
if the two points of view are irreconcilable, yet on the other hand
neither would exist without the other, and they melt into each
other by a process which we cannot grasp. If we insist upon
thinking of the soul as something *wholly* isolated, as *merely* a
substance with states, then it is hopeless to attempt to arrive at
the conception of other souls. For if there are other souls, we must
think of our own soul as more intimately attached to its own body
than to the rest of its environment; we detach and idealize some
of its states. We thus pass to the point of view from which the
soul is the entelechy of its body. It is this transition from one point
of view to another which is known to Mr Bradley's readers as
transcendence. It is the failure to deal adequately with transcendence, or even to recognize the true nature of the problem,
which makes Leibniz appear so fantastic, and puts him sometimes
to such awkward shifts.

Thus Leibniz, while he makes the soul the entelechy of the
body, is forced to have recourse to the theory of the dominant
monad. Now I contend that if one recognizes two points of view,
which are irreconcilable and yet melt into each other, this theory
is quite superfluous. It is really an attempt to preserve the reality
of the external world at the same time that it is denied, which is
perhaps the attempt of all pan-psychism: to substitute for two
concepts which have at least a relative validity in practice —
consciousness and matter — one which is less useful and consequently less significant — animated matter. So far as my body is
merely an adjective of my soul, I suppose that it needs no outside
explanation; and so far as it possesses an independent reality, it is
quite unnecessary to say that this is because it is compounded of
elements which are adjectives of other souls or monads. Leibniz
has here done no more than to add to the concepts of psychical
and physical a third and otiose concept.

The monad in fact combines, or attempts to combine, several
points of view in one. Because Leibniz tries to run these different

Leibniz' Monads and Bradley's Finite Centres

aspects together, and at the same time refuses to recognize that the independence and isolation of the monads is only a relative and partial aspect, he lets himself in for the most unnecessary of his mysteries — the pre-established harmony. Bradley turns the Absolute to account for the same purpose. 'The one Absolute' knows itself and realizes itself in and through finite centres. 'For rejecting a higher experience,' Mr Bradley says, 'in which appearances are transformed, I can find no reason. . . .'* But what we do know is that we are able to pass from one point of view to another, that we are compelled to do so, and that the different aspects more or less hang together. For rejecting a higher experience there may be no reason. But that this higher experience explains the lower is at least open to doubt.

Mr Bradley's monadism is in some ways a great advance beyond Leibniz'. Its technical excellence is impeccable. It unquestionably presents clearness where in Leibniz we find confusion. I am not sure that the ultimate puzzle is any more frankly faced, or that divine intervention plays any smaller part. Mr Bradley is a much more skilful, a much more finished philosopher than Leibniz. He has the melancholy grace, the languid mastery, of the late product. He has expounded one type of philosophy with such consummate ability that it will probably not survive him. In Leibniz there are possibilities. He has the permanence of the pre-Socratics, of all imperfect things.

* *Truth and Reality,* p. 413.

Selected Bibliography

Only those books and articles to which Mr Eliot has made reference are listed here and, wherever specific pagination is involved, the editions cited are those which he used and those to which the pagination of his references therefore applies. Inasmuch as the 1893 edition of Bradley's *Appearance and Reality* and the 1912 edition of Russell's *The Problems of Philosophy* which he used are now both out of print, Mr Eliot's references to these two volumes have been transposed to those of the 1946 and 1962 editions, respectively. It is these two current editions which are therefore listed below and to which Mr Eliot's references now apply. Bradley's *Collected Essays* has been added to the Bibliography inasmuch as several of the essays to which Mr Eliot refers may be found there, and because this volume is more readily accessible than are the early issues of *Mind* in which the essays originally appeared.

Anne C. Bolgan

Adams, George P. 'Mind as Form and as Activity.' *The Philosophical Review* XXII (1913) 265–83.

Alexander, S. 'Mental Activity in Willing and in Ideas.' *Proceedings of the Aristotelian Society* New Series IX (1908–1909) 1–40.

———. 'On Sensations and Images.' *Proceedings of the Aristotelian Society* New Series X (1909–1910) 1–35.

———. 'Foundations and Sketch-plan of a Conational Psychology.' *The British Journal of Psychology* IX (1911) 239–267.

———. 'The Method of Metaphysics and the Categories.' *Mind* XXI (1912) 1–20.

Bosanquet, Bernard. *The Essentials of Logic.* London: Macmillan and Company, 1895.

Selected Bibliography

Bosanquet, Bernard. *Logic, or the Morphology of Knowledge.* In Two Volumes. Oxford: Clarendon Press, 1911.

——. *The Principle of Individuality and Value.* London: Macmillan and Company Limited, 1912.

Bradley, F. H. *The Principles of Logic.* London: Kegan Paul, Trench, and Company, 1883.

——. *Appearance and Reality.* Oxford: Clarendon Press, 1946.

——. *Essays on Truth and Reality.* Oxford: Clarendon Press, 1914.

——. *Collected Essays.* In Two Volumes. Oxford: Clarendon Press, 1935.

——. 'Some Remarks on Memory and Inference.' *Mind* VIII (1899) 145–66.

——. 'A Defense of Phenomenalism in Psychology.' *Mind* IX (1900) 26–45. Reprinted in *Collected Essays* II 364–86.

——. 'On Active Attention.' *Mind* XI (1902) 1–30. Reprinted in *Collected Essays* II 408–43.

——. 'The Definition of Will (I).' *Mind* XI (1902) 437–69. Reprinted in *Collected Essays* II 476–514.

——. 'The Definition of Will (II).' *Mind* XII (1903) 145–76. Reprinted in *Collected Essays* II 515–51.

——. 'The Definition of Will (III).' *Mind* XIII (1904) 1–37. Reprinted in *Collected Essays* II 552–94.

——. 'On Floating Ideas and the Imaginary.' *Mind* XV (1906) 445–72. Reprinted in *Essays on Truth and Reality* 28–64.

Brunnhofer, Hermann. *Giordano Bruno's Lehre vom Kleinsten als die Quelle der Prästabilirten Harmonie von Leibnitz.* Leipzig: Rauert & Rocco, 1890.

Burnet, John. *Greek Philosophy.* London: Macmillan and Company, 1914.

Couturat, Louis. *Opuscules et fragments inédits de Leibniz.* Paris: Alcan, 1903.

Dillmann, Eduard. *Eine neue Darstellung der Leibnizischen Monadenlehre auf Grund der Quellen.* Leipzig: Reisland, 1891.

Dumville, Benjamin. 'The Standpoint of Psychology.' *Proceedings of the Aristotelian Society* New Series XI (1910–1911) 41–79.

Selected Bibliography

Foucher de Careil, Alexandre L. *Réfutation inédite de Spinoza par Leibniz*. Paris: Librairie philosophique de Ladrange, 1854.

———. *Leibniz, la philosophie juive, et la cabale*. Paris: August Durand, 1861.

Gerber, Gustav. *Die Sprache und das Erkennen*. Berlin: R. Gaertners Verlogsbuchhandlung, 1884.

Hicks, G. Dawes. 'The Relation of Subject and Object from the Point of View of Psychological Development.' *Proceedings of the Aristotelian Society* New Series VIII (1907–1908) 160–214.

———. 'Mr. G. E. Moore on "The Subject-Matter of Psychology".' *Proceedings of the Aristotelian Society* New Series X (1909–1910) 232–88.

Hoernlé, R. F. Alfred. 'Image, Idea and Meaning.' *Mind* XVI (1907) 70–100.

Höfler, Alois. *Psychologie*. Wien und Prag: F. Tempsky, 1897.

Holt, Edwin B. and Others. *The New Realism: Cooperative Studies in Philosophy*. New York: The Macmillan Company, 1912.

James, William. *Essays in Radical Empiricism*. London: Longmans, Green, and Company, 1912.

Jerusalem, Wilhelm. *Die Urtheilsfunction*. Wien und Leipzig: Braumüller, 1895.

Joachim, Harold. *The Nature of Truth*. Oxford: Clarendon Press, 1906.

———. 'Psychical Process.' *Mind* XVIII (1909) 65–83.

Joseph, H. W. B. 'The Psychological Explanation of the Development of the Perception of External Objects (I).' *Mind* XIX (1910) 305–21.

———. 'The Psychological Explanation of the Development of the Perception of External Objects (II).' *Mind* XIX (1910) 457–69.

———. 'The Psychological Explanation of the Development of the Perception of External Objects (III). (Reply to Prof. Stout).' *Mind* XX (1911) 161–80.

Kabitz, Willy. *Die Philosophie des jungen Leibniz*. Heidelberg: Carl Winter's Universitätsbuchhandlung, 1909.

Selected Bibliography

Leibniz, Gottfried Wilhelm. *The Monadology and Other Philosophical Writings*. Translated with an Introduction and Notes by Robert Latta. Oxford: Clarendon Press, 1898.

———. *Discourse on Metaphysics Correspondence with Arnauld, and Monadology*. With an Introduction by Paul Janet and Translated from the originals by George R. Montgomery. Chicago: The Open Court Publishing Company, 1902.

Lévy-Bruhl, Lucien. *Les Fonctions Mentales dans Les Sociétés Inférieures*. Paris: Alcan, 1910.

Lipps, Theodor. *Vom Fühlen, Wollen und Denken: Versuch einer Theorie des Willens*. Zweite, vollig umgearbeitete Auflage. Heft 13 und 14 der *Schriften der Gesellschaft für psychologische Forschung*. Leipzig: Barth, 1907.

———. 'Inhalt und Gegenstand; Psychologie und Logik.' *Sitzungsberichte der philosophisch-philologischen und der historischen Klasse der K. B. Akademie der Wissenschaften zu München* (1905) 511–669.

McTaggart, J. M. E. *Studies in the Hegelian Dialetic*. Cambridge: University Press, 1896.

Meinong, Alexis. *Über die Erfahrungsgrundlagen unseres Wissens*. Heft 6 der *Abhandlungen zur Didaktik und Philosophie der Naturwissenschaft*. Herausgegeben von F. Poske in Berlin, A. Höfler in Prag und E. Grimsehl in Hamburg. Berlin: Springer, 1906.

———. *Über Annahmen*. Zweite, umgearbeitete Auflage. Leipzig: Barth, 1910.

Merz, John Theodore. *Leibniz*. London: William Blackwood and Sons, 1884.

Messer, August. *Einführung in die Erkenntnistheorie*. Band 118 der *Philosophischen Bibliothek*. Leipzig: Meiner, 1909.

———. *Psychologie*. Stuttgart: Deutsche Verlogs-Anstalt, 1914.

Moore, G. E. 'The Nature of Judgement.' *Mind* VIII (1899) 176–193.

———. 'The Subject-Matter of Psychology.' *Proceedings of the Aristotelian Society* New Series X (1909–1910) 36–62.

Selected Bibliography

Nettleship, Richard Lewis. *Philosophical Lectures and Remains.* Edited, with a Biographical Sketch by A. C. Bradley and G. R. Benson. In Two Volumes. London: Macmillan and Company Limited, 1897.

Nolen, D. *Quid Leibnizius Aristoteli debuerit.* Paris: Germer Balliére Bibliopola, 1875.

Nunn, T. Percy. 'Are Secondary Qualities Independent of Perception?' *Proceedings of the Aristotelian Society* New Series X (1909–1910) 191–218.

Peirce, Charles Sanders. *Collected Papers.* Eight Volumes. Edited by Charles Hartshorne and Paul Weiss. (Volumes 7 and 8 edited by Arthur W. Burks.) Cambridge: Harvard University Press, 1931–1958.

Prichard, H. A. *Kant's Theory of Knowledge.* Oxford: Clarendon Press, 1909.

———. 'A Criticism of the Psychologists' Treatment of Knowledge.' *Mind* XVI (1907) 27–53.

Ross, W. D. editor. *The Works of Aristotle.* Translated into English. Volume I *Analytica Posteriora.* Volume III *De Anima.* Volume VIII *Metaphysica.* Oxford: Clarendon Press, 1908.

Rubin, Salomon. *Die Erkenntnistheorie Maimons in ihrem Verhältnis zu Cartesius, Leibnitz, Hume und Kant.* Band 7 der *Berner Studien zur Philosophie und ihrer Geschichte.* Herausgegeben von Dr Ludwig Stein. Bern: Steiger & Cie, 1897.

Russell, Bertrand. *A Critical Exposition of the Philosophy of Leibniz.* Cambridge: University Press, 1900.

———. *The Problems of Philosophy.* London: Oxford University Press, 1962.

———. 'Recent Work on the Philosophy of Leibniz.' *Mind* XII (1903) 177–201.

———. 'Meinong's Theory of Complexes and Assumptions (I), (II), and (III).' *Mind* XIII (1904) 204–19, 336–54, and 509–524, respectively.

———. 'On Denoting.' *Mind* XIV (1905) 479–93.

Selected Bibliography

Russell, Bertrand. 'Knowledge by Acquaintance and Knowledge by Description.' *Proceedings of the Aristotelian Society* New Series XI (1910–1911) 108–28. Not to be confused with the essay of the same title in *The Problems of Philosophy*.

————. 'On the Relations of Universals and Particulars.' *Proceedings of the Aristotelian Society* New Series XII (1911–1912) 1–24.

Sigwart, Christoph. *Logic*. In Two Volumes. Second Edition, Revised and Enlarged. Translated by Helen Dendy. London: Swan Sonnenschein and Company, 1895.

Stout, G. F. *Analytic Psychology*. In Two Volumes. London: Swan Sonnenschein and Company, 1896.

————. *A Manual of Psychology*. London: University Correspondence College Press, 1899.

————. 'Mr. Prichard's Criticism of Psychology.' *Mind* XVI (1907) 236–43.

————. 'Are Presentations Mental or Physical? A Reply to Professor Alexander.' *Proceedings of the Aristotelian Society* New Series IX (1908–1909) 226–47.

————. 'The Object of Thought and Real Being.' *Proceedings of the Aristotelian Society* New Series XI (1910–1911) 187–205.

————. 'Reply to Mr. Joseph.' *Mind* XX (1911) 1–14.

Titchener, Edward Bradford. *Lectures on the Elementary Psychology of Feeling and Attention*. New York: The Macmillan Company, 1908.

————. *A Text-book of Psychology*. In Two Parts. New York: The Macmillan Company, 1909.

Ward, James. 'Psychology.' *Encyclopaedia Britannica*. Eleventh Edition XXII 547–604.

Wendt, Emil. *Die Entwickelung der Leibnizischen Monadenlehre bis zum Jahre 1695*. Berlin: Weidmannsche Buchhandlung, 1886.

Witasek, Stephan. *Grundlinien der Psychologie*. Leipzig: Meiner, 1908.

Wodehouse, Helen. *The Presentation of Reality*. Cambridge: University Press, 1910.

Index

Index

Index